A Primer of Fly-Fishing

First fly fishing lesson
was on 2/4/92
(private lesson)

A Primer of Fly-Fishing

Roderick Haig-Brown

Illustrated by Louis Darling

Douglas & McIntyre
Vancouver/Toronto

Frank Amato Publications
Portland, Oregon

Douglas & McIntyre Ltd.
1615 Venables Street
Vancouver, British Columbia V5L 2H1

Canadian Cataloguing in Publication Data
Haig-Brown, Roderick L., 1908-1976.
A primer of fly-fishing

   Originally published: New York: Morrow, 1964
   Includes index.
   ISBN 0-88894-349-0

   1. Fly fishing. I. Title.
   SH456.H22 1982   799.1'2   C82-091047-3

Published in the United States of America by
Frank Amato Publications, Box 82112,
Portland, Oregon 97282

Printed and bound in Canada by D. W. Friesen & Sons Ltd.

CONTENTS

INTRODUCTION

Good sense and gentle wisdom rooted in long experience never go out of fashion. And when they are couched in the measured and thoughtful prose of Roderick Haig-Brown, such qualities become doubly appealing. Such is the case with *A Primer of Fly-Fishing*. It is a basic but wise book, and it retains those rich qualities of a master's prose while yet dwelling on what might be called the less poetic, more mundane aspects of angling.

All of Haig-Brown's books instruct — with the instruction that is inevitable when one fishes in a great man's boots with him — but

A Primer instructs most directly. As such — as with all books of instruction in a time of change — it is the one book among Haig-Brown's major titles that would be in most danger of not wearing well over the years. Oddly, this has not happened. It has worn exceptionally well. Though much has changed in the world of fly-fishing since 1964, when this book was written, its basic truths remain valid and pristine.

What better advice with which to start than a chapter called "On the Virtues of Worms"? He says, and he is surely right, "It usually starts with a worm, and it may well be that there is still no adequate substitute for such a start." Use of the worm teaches "observation, stealth, and ingenuity," a knowledge of fish habits and habitat, quick reflexes — and these and other quintessential skills become part of what a young angler will take with him along what Haig-Brown calls the "natural development" towards fly-fishing.

And the advice on rods and reels, lines, leaders and hooks, flies, knots, casting, dry- and wet-fly fishing, playing a fish, fishing in lakes and streams and salt water, fly-tying, tradition, and even ethics — all this remains fundamentally sound and thoughtful instruction, of the kind every fly-fisherman (beginning and more experienced) should read and then re-read periodically. It is no mean feat to present the practical aspects of a very complex and palpable activity like fly-fishing in an absolutely helpful, lucid, and distilled manner, without being condescending. The book is as clear as a mountain brook; and it is a wonder that so much has been said, so much territory covered, in under two hundred pages.

Of course the particular seventeen or eighteen years since this book was written have been unlike any comparable period. The changes have been dramatic and far-reaching in their implications. We have been benefitted by science — and been beset upon by it — in the most astonishing ways. Line designations have changed from the old (and to my mind confusing) letter system to an absolutely simple system of numbers; a variety of startlingly effective fly patterns — using new designs, new materials, new concepts of imitation — have evolved; reels may have stayed rather the same but graphite and boron have revolutionized fly-rod construction; prices — in this book still modest — have in some instances sky-rocketed; and there has been a vast broadening of fly-fishing's frontiers in fields like fly-fishing in salt water.

But none of these changes — which have not been adjusted in the present text — seriously affect the virtues of this marvelous book. This is still the first book I would give to a novice fly-fisherman; it is still the best basic introduction to fly-fishing; and it is still a standard for anyone who would understand how best to present in word what eventually must be learned by hand and eye. (Sadly, we now have a generation of technically excellent and even innovative anglers, many of whom have not learned the first syllable of what the great Haig-Brown knew about writing — and we have muddled, repetitive, and pedestrian books that are greatly muddying the water of fly-fishing literature.)

We miss Roderick Haig-Brown — that wise and gentle man who touched our hearts and defined the fly-fishing experience with unsurpassable skill. We shall not have his like again. But we still have gems like this book, where one part of him lives and instructs us still — and that makes it a special treat to have *A Primer of Fly-Fishing* back in print at last. I may have grandchildren before too much longer, and I shall want to give them a copy of this book, to introduce them to a pastime that enriches us beyond measure.

Nick Lyons

CHAPTER ONE

On the Virtues of Worms

IT USUALLY STARTS with a worm, and it may well be that there is still no adequate substitute for such a start. With a limber pole, a length of line, a simple or nonexistent reel and a worm on a hook, a boy is quite severely limited. Observation, stealth and ingenuity must play a very large part in any success, and these, taken in large doses when one is very young, lead to a knowledge of fish habits and an understanding of water that are never forgotten.

Given an outfit that will cast the full width of a river and sweep it from side to side with a variety of lures and baits, there is less need to be stealthy, ingenious, observant, less need to learn.

Not that there is any harm in starting directly with a fly, except that for a very young boy the demands may be a little too great. The muscles have to reach a certain level of development and sophistication before they can master the skills and rhythms of casting a fly, and it can be discouraging to watch the easy triumph of one's contemporaries with lures and bait while the fly goes unrewarded. But when a boy is twelve or fourteen, and even before that in very small waters such as brooks and beaver ponds, the elements of fly-fishing can be mastered and real learning can begin.

But I still think of the worm as a great teacher, and a word or two about it is not out of place in a book about fly-fishing. The worm I am thinking of is a strong, healthy creature that has been kept several days in damp moss to clean himself and harden his skin. He could, perhaps, equally well be a hellgrammite, a caddis grub, a caterpillar or some other natural food of trout, but the worm is everywhere easily found, so he is usually the young angler's choice.

Such a worm, then, one that is hard, bright and brilliantly red, should be fished on an offset hook of not too large a size—not larger than No. 6, better No. 8 or No. 10—which means he should not be too large a worm. A leader of four pounds' breaking strain is about right, except when the water is very low and clear, and a few split shot are enough to weight the worm and make casting easy.

Any limber pole with a length of line from the tip will fish this worm effectively, but an old, soft fly rod with a simple reel and fifty yards of ten-pound monafilament is most practical. So equipped, a boy can go to any trout water and start learning. When the water is high, in spring and early summer, there is no great difficulty. He can cast his worm in and let the current carry it into the more or less likely spots. Learning will come quite quickly. Too much weight (too many split shot) is easier to cast, but catches bottom; too little will not get the worm down to the fish. Some spots are more productive than others, and these have recognizable similarities. Some places are good for big fish, some for small fish, some are a waste of time. There is a difference between the feel of the bottom and the feel of a fish mouthing the worm. There is a way of raising the rod top firmly enough to strike the hook into the fish, yet not so firmly that it breaks the leader. There is a right moment for this, and a wrong moment. One must be quicker with a little fish than with a big one.

All these things are part of any type of fishing and all, learned in youth, will find their echoes in later fishing, with the special advantage that they have become part of the fisherman and are used without conscious thought. But the testing time and the real learning time, even with the worm, is in summer and fall, when the water is low and clear. It is best now to work upstream, approaching the fish from behind, keeping the head low and the rod low, stalking the fish rather than searching for them, sneaking up on the likely places rather than simply searching through them. The leader may be finer, the shot fewer, both hook and worm smaller still. The cast is a delicate sidearm swing that slides the worm forward through the air, drawing a few coils of loose line from the left hand, and plops it in at the head of the run. It comes drifting back. The line is slowly and carefully recovered through the rings of the rod, keeping pace but never pulling on the worm. Suddenly it stops, holds against the current. It is time to strike and the fish is there.

None of this is easy. In its way it is more difficult than fishing the upstream nymph and much more difficult than fishing the dry fly under similar conditions. The casting is much more difficult because any roughness will jerk the worm off the hook; the gentle sidearm swing makes accuracy difficult and any real distance impossible, so the approach must be doubly cunning and careful. The only advantage is in the bait itself, which, being alive and edible, may be more enticing to a wary fish than feathers and wool on a hook. But in truth, when he has developed this far the boy might as well or better be fishing a fly. He is ready for it and the worm has little more to teach him.

The natural development of any fisherman, except possibly the big-game fisherman, is towards fly-fishing. Some hesitate because it seems difficult or expensive or complicated. Yet it is none of these things. Some feel it is ineffective, that they will catch fewer fish; yet under the right conditions— and the variety is very wide—fly-fishing can be highly effective and under some conditions it can be more effective than any other method. There is also a perverse notion that fly-fishing is somehow undemocratic. It is undoubtedly the best and finest of all forms of fishing, making the strongest demands on the attention and understanding of its followers and yielding in return the greatest and richest rewards;

but in this it is exactly the same as the best in music, painting, literature or anything else. Men from every conceivable walk of life are fly-fishermen, and good ones, for nothing but individual choice limits membership in the brotherhood.

Fly-fishing has a great literature and a long tradition; in 1486, when Dame Juliana Berners' first descriptions of fly-fishing gear and methods were printed, it was already a well-established sport, with standard fly patterns based on a fair understanding of entomology and of the seasons for the different flies. Yet it is a sport that has grown only slowly and gradually over the centuries. Two hundred years after Berners, in the fly-fishing section of *The Compleat Angler*, Charles Cotton did much to define the current techniques of the fly-fisher and to shape his future philosophy of observant gentleness and joyful relaxation in the lovely surroundings of the stream. More than two hundred years later still, in the late nineteenth and early twentieth centuries, most of the modern techniques were developed to advanced perfection and all the frantic excitements and mechanical ingenuities of the mid-twentieth century have done little to change the sport significantly. This is one of the charms of fly-fishing. Within a day or two Charles Cotton could be using modern gear and methods as skillfully as the best of us; and within a day or two most of us could be taking a few fish with Cotton's own gear on the seventeenth-century Dove, though we might find his horehair leaders rather less dependable than today's nylon.

A fly-fisherman is usually caricatured as a poor little man, entangled, festooned and overburdened with the assorted paraphernalia of his craft. It is true, I'm afraid, that we do tend to hang a lot of stuff about ourselves, "just in case it might be needed." But in truth the essentials of fly-fishing are extremely simple, and this is another of its charms. Rod, reel and line, these are the essentials that any angler must carry. Add to them a couple of leaders and a small box of flies slipped into the pocket and the fly-fisherman is fully equipped—no swivels or leads or spare hooks, no boxes of tangled lures; above all, no bait cans with their messy contents waiting to be impaled on the hook from time to time throughout the day. Complicate it as we will with spare lines, special fly boxes, fly dope and extra gadgets innumerable and inconsequential, the essential simplicity remains. We intend to take our fish with a few strands of wool or tinsel, a few feather strips or a wisp of hair tied on to a hook.

Casting with any type of gear can be fun, but here, too, the fly-fisherman has enormous advantages. He depends only upon the flex of his rod and the weight of his line; the rest is himself. He is forced into a performance of grace and skill that is an immense satisfaction in itself. He cannot cast as far as the bait fisherman and he has much greater problems with overhanging trees and bushes, but there are solutions for all such problems and satisfaction in the skill and knowledge that produce them.

Seeing the fish is no small part of fishing pleasure, and one of the angler's keenest excitements is in watching a good fish come up to strike the hook. Inevitably this is possible far more often in fly-fishing than in any other form of angling, since the fly is usually near the surface if not actually on it. When the fish strikes a fly there are only the rod and line between fish and fisherman, no weights, no clumsy lure to impede movement, no bait hook fast in the gills or the gullet. The fly-caught fish is free to do his best, and nearly always, when he is brought to beach or bank, the fly-fisherman can release him without difficulty or damage.

I have emphasized the essential simplicity of fly-fishing because people are inclined to think it is a highly special art, full of complexities and mysteries. I would not deny that the sport has great complexities, many subtleties and refinements, perhaps even its own special mysteries. But these need not deter or concern the beginner or the practical fisherman who wants nothing more than to go out on lake or stream, cast a fly and catch a few fish. One can be a very effective and contented performer without going beyond the simplicities. But the complexities and subtleties are there for anyone who wishes to explore them; a lifetime will not unravel all their possibilities and delights, and this, perhaps, is why so many able and distinguished men remain dedicated fly-fishermen so long as they can hold a rod or go out along the streams.

Finally, the surroundings of fly-fishing are nearly always delightful. Mountain lakes or lowland lakes, rushing streams or quiet meadow streams, tidal estuaries or salt-water shallows, all have their own special charms and moods. Spring and summer and fall are a fly-fisherman's usual times, and he moves quietly through them, disturbing little, seeing much if his eyes are receptive. Some of the early fishing writers, understanding well the attractions of their sport and its surroundings, were concerned at the thought that their books might fall into the hands of "idle persons" and make them still more idle. I have no such concern. If I can persuade any man to idle away a day on a stream or a lake when he should be doing something much more important, I am satisfied I have done him and the world a service. At any given moment in the world's history there has always been an excess of people busy doing important things, and there always will be.

It is with all these thoughts in mind that I have taken it upon myself to explain, as best I can, the simplicities of fly-fishing and perhaps a few of its lesser complexities. It is by no means a difficult sport to learn, but a little instruction and explanation can shorten the learning immensely and make a competent performer instead of a frustrated beginner. To be happy and at ease in any active sport one needs to acquire a few fundamental skills, and it is well also to have some understanding of the various tools or implements and their uses, the various methods and their purposes. The object of such learning is not necessarily to become expert, though some may wish to go on to that distant stage; it is to be comfortable enough to find enjoyment and at the same time to be sufficiently aware of what one is doing to sharpen the enjoyment. Once that level of performance and understanding is achieved, any man can build upon it and make the sport his own. In fly-fishing it is very easily achieved.

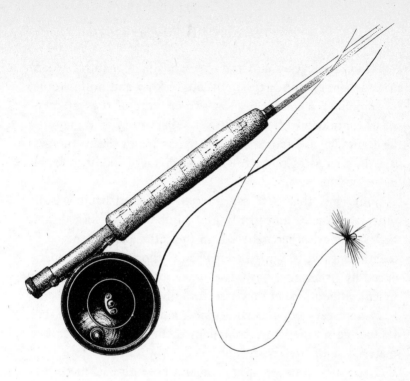

CHAPTER TWO

Rods and Reels

THE MODERN FLY ROD is a beautifully designed piece of equipment, developed over hundreds of years by enthusiasts, both amateur and professional. No doubt there will be further improvements as new materials are developed and new designs are fitted to them, but it is difficult to imagine that any such improvements will be significant to most fishermen, except possibly in the matter of price and some small degree of comfort.

A hundred years ago rods were made of natural woods such as ash, greenheart, lancewood, hickory and hollow cane, or sometimes a combination of two or more of these. Greenheart continued well into the twentieth century, and may still be found in use today, though it has many disadvantages: it is heavier, less powerful and much more likely to break under sudden strain.

Split cane, that is to say, specially selected bamboo split into six segments and firmly glued into a single stick, began to displace all other materials in the latter part of the nineteenth century, and it still remains the choice of most experienced fly-fishermen. Only two other materials have given it much competition: hollow steel and fiber glass. Hollow-steel rods were very popular and some good ones were made, but they have nothing to recommend them over the other two materials and may be forgotten.

The choice between split cane and fiber glass is more difficult. A well-made split-cane rod is a wonderfully sensitive instrument, a thing of beauty and value even apart from its performance. Rodmakers have learned to heat-treat and harden their cane, giving it a steely liveliness and power; more recently they have learned to impregnate it with plastics so that it is practically impervious to weather and wear and age. Every cane rod has its own individuality, made up of tiny variations in the handwork and materials that go into it, and an experienced fisherman can choose among them until he has one that seems to suit his special need. All these qualities have a special appeal, supported by the natural conservatism that quite properly makes old anglers cling to old ways and familiar equipment. We remember the days of our youth, when split cane was supreme and unchallenged. Like the old greenheart men before us, we do not care to believe that any newfangled thing can adequately replace it.

The first fiber-glass rods that appeared on the market immediately after World War II certainly encouraged conservative thinking. They were poorly designed and poorly finished, with cheap and flimsy ferrules and reel fittings and improperly spaced guides of poor quality. No self-respecting fly-fisherman could have been expected to give them a second glance. All that is changed. One can now buy glass rods of excellent design and workmanship, well fitted and well finished in every way. The best of them will do anything a good split-cane rod will do, and do it really well. They may not have quite the same feel as cane, but even that is a matter of opinion. They may not offer the fisherman his choice among subtle variations of action, but this, I suspect, is small loss since any competent fisherman can adjust himself to the peculiarities of whatever rod he is using in a short spell of fishing. The important points are these: a good glass fly rod costs only about half as much as a cane rod of similar quality, it is likely to be a shade lighter in proportion to its power and it will stand far more abuse. Any beginning fly-fisherman, young or old, should start out with one of these and decide later, as his experience develops, whether the virtues of split cane are great enough to justify a change. If price is a serious consideration, they probably never will be.

The next matters of choice in a fly rod are length and weight. Length is fairly simple; most modern fly rods are between eight and nine feet long, and these are the most practical lengths for all normal purposes. Weight is more difficult because the important thing here is not the weight itself but how it is distributed through the rod—it is easy to understand, for instance, that a rod wih a heavy tip and a light butt will have an entirely different action and performance from that of a rod with a light tip and heavy butt, even though both may have the same total weight. The total weight of a rod, including its fittings, is simply a rough guide in selection. The final selection must be made by the feel and balance of the rod in the hand.

While there are good practical fly rods of seven feet and less and ten feet or more, these are for somewhat special purposes. A seven-foot rod is very pleasant to use for small fish in small waters, and even a beginner who was going to limit himself to such conditions might do well to choose one; a rod of this size may also be the choice of an expert who wishes to test his skill against larger fish in larger waters, but it is not a logical choice for the general run of fly-fishing conditions. Similarly, a rod of ten feet or over may be a logical choice for an experienced fisherman who is going to use large flies for Atlantic Salmon or salt-water fish. But it takes a good deal of skill and power to use such rods effectively; they can be quite tiring in use and they are a nuisance in traveling along brushy streams or casting in cramped conditions.

For summer and fall, when the fly is usually fished on or close to the surface, an eight-foot rod weighing about four ounces is very pleasant indeed to use. A good one will throw up to seventy-five or eighty feet of line and with care and patience will handle any fish that is likely to take hold of a fly. A rod of this size may well be the choice of a fisherman who is going to fish only the smaller eastern streams, but it is perhaps a little small and light for more general purposes. A few inches more length, for instance, is always useful in lake fishing and a little more power is a help in lifting the deeply sunk lines and large flies one often uses in the spring.

A nine-foot fiber-glass rod, which should weigh five ounces or a little more, is surprisingly powerful. Unless one is going to be using wet flies as large as 1/0 and larger or dry flies larger than size 6, or consistently fighting heavy winds and fish of over five pounds, it is probably unnecessarily powerful.

A GENERAL-PURPOSE FLY ROD

This suggests that the ideal general-purpose rod is somewhere between these two, and I believe it is. Largely by coincidence, I find that the three rods I have used most consistently over the past thirty years have all been eight and three-quarter feet long. They are cane rods; two of them weigh five ounces each and the third, which is the least powerful, weighs five and three-eighths ounces. These rods are pleasant to use, sensitive enough for trout from ten inches up to ten pounds or more; they will cast dry flies up to size 6 and wet flies up to size 1 without feeling clumsy or awkward; they are long enough for lake fishing and strong enough to lift a sunk line and throw it well out against adverse conditions.

It so happens that I have never owned an eight-and-a-half-foot rod, yet I cannot believe that the extra three inches on the rods I have just described are of any real significance. Rods of eight and a half feet are much more easily found than rods of eight and three-quarter feet, so it seems wise to settle on one of these eight-and-a-half-footers, weighing perhaps four and a half ounces and made of fiber glass, as the ideal general-purpose rod for anyone who has never owned a fly rod before. The rod should have a fairly stiff action and a pleasant feel of movement in the hand. Butt and tip guides should be of good quality agate or else tungsten steel. Intermediate rings should be of the snake type, and there should be a screw-grip reel fitting large enough to take a four-inch-diameter reel. Two-piece rods are perfectly satisfactory and generally easier to find, though any two-piece rod of more than eight feet is sometimes a nuisance when traveling. The present cost of a good fiber-glass rod to these specifications should be between thirty and sixty dollars. A cane rod of comparable quality would be harder to find and would certainly cost between fifty and a hundred dollars.

So much for the general specifications of a rod that will cover nearly all types of North American fly-fishing well enough, most of them very well indeed. The final test is how it feels in the hand. A fisherman of moderate experience can try this in the store by fitting on a reel and working the rod in his casting hand, though he would do better to try it outside with a line of the right size if it is possible to do so. The beginner must trust an experienced friend, the more experienced the better, though he would still be wise to make the final selection himself from among three or four rods that his friend decides are satisfactory.

FLY REELS

The reel is not a vital part of a fly-fisherman's equipment —that is, he can get by with almost anything that will reel up his line for him or run it out under pressure from a fish. But a good reel will last a lifetime with reasonable care, while a cheap one is less pleasant to use and may have to be replaced after a season or two. A fly reel should be as simple as possible, with a large diameter drum, narrow between the plates, for quick recovery of line, and an ordinary pawl and ratchet drag, preferably adjustable. In my opinion, automatic reels, auxiliary drags and multiplying effects are all pointless, more likely to give trouble than ease or comfort and certain to detract from the direct and natural feel of a fish when one is hooked.

The best fly reels, apart from very costly handmade jobs which are usually more expensive than they should be, are English made. The drums run from about three to four inches in diameter with a width of something less than an inch between the plates, and weights are usually from about six to nine ounces. Smaller and lighter reels are obtainable, but these are not essential for the size and weight of rod I have described. A fly reel loaded with line should have weight enough to bring the point of balance of the rod an inch or two forward of the cork grip; for general trout fishing the reel should have room without crowding for the fly line and fifty yards of backing line. Where fish of three or four pounds or more are to be expected, at least a hundred yards of backing is good insurance, which suggests a reel of about three and seven-eighths inches in diameter with about

seven eighths of an inch between the plates, but these meas-
urements are suggested only as a rough guide.

Reels of this size and type should cost something between
ten and twenty-five dollars. Cheaper reels can be found, but
are not likely to be satisfactory. A complete fly-fishing outfit, with rod, reel and tapered line of workable quality, can
be bought for a total of fifteen dollars or less, but I am trying to suggest rather a good, efficient outfit that will serve a
fly-fisherman under all sorts of conditions for many years
and leave him at a practical disadvantage with no one. Fifty
dollars will buy a rod and reel to do this. A good fly line,
which is the business part of the outfit, will cost another ten
or fifteen dollars, but that is another story and another
chapter.

CHAPTER THREE

Fly Lines

I HAD NOT MEANT to treat so lengthily and seriously of rods and reels, but no fisherman or hunter can resist a certain measure of enthusiasm and affection for his tools, and these two, fly rods and fly reels, have been brought to an astonishing perfection and beauty in the course of many generations. I do not want to suggest that there is any mystery or difficulty in this—the choosing of a satisfactory rod is really a very simple matter—but enjoyment of the tools of angling is certainly an important part of the pleasure of the sport, and it is impossible to discuss them at all without suggesting this.

While a good rod is an important piece of equipment, a good line, well matched to the rod, is essential. It is the line that gets the work out of the rod in fly-fishing. If it is too heavy, it will overpower the rod and spoil its performance; if it is too light to flex the rod properly at the beginning and end of the cast, it simply does not develop any power at all and the fisherman is left ineffectively flailing the air. There is a measure of tolerance in this matching of the rod to the line. Since a fisherman normally expects to be able to cast effectively and accurately at all distances from fifteen or twenty feet up to seventy-five feet or more with the same rod and line, there must be. But even so, the better the match the better and more comfortable the performance will be, so it is well to understand something about fly lines.

FLY-LINE MATERIALS

Most modern fly lines are made of silk, dacron or nylon. Dacron lines have a high specific gravity and are generally used to sink the fly deep in the water. Silk lines will float or sink equally well, depending on whether or not they are greased. Nylon lines are light in proportion to their thickness and are often made lighter by introducing air into the dressing, in which case they are called floaters.

Silk is probably the best of the three materials. It casts beautifully, forces well into a wind, has no tendency to crack its dressing by stretch and will develop a fine suppleness under proper care. Well greased, it will float all day. Without grease it sinks quite readily, though it soaks up water and becomes too heavy in time. Silk lines do need some care. They must be taken off the reel and dried after each day's fishing and they must be carefully greased and polished to be at their best. When not in use they should be taken off the reel and hung in loose coils in a dry, cool, dark place. Cared for in this way, silk lines should last indefinitely and improve with use. But they are temperamental things, and under mistreatment may become sticky and stiff and useless, or even rotten, after a few seasons.

Nylon lines usually have a very smooth finish and are supple and pleasant to use. Because of their lighter weight in proportion to diameter, they may be a little more difficult to cast against a strong wind, but the difference is scarcely noticeable. The "floaters" will keep floating pretty well indefinitely without greasing, though a light greasing floats them higher and sometimes prevents the front end of the taper from sinking. For a fisherman who does all his fishing with floating flies, nymphs or wet flies fished close to the surface, these lines probably are best. They need little care, though it is well to give them a chance to dry by stripping them off the reel at the end of a day's fishing. But they have one very bad fault. Nylon stretches excessively, and the dressing, especially at the forward tip of the taper, cracks away from the line after a few weeks of hard fishing. I have owned several nylon lines and have never yet been able to make one last through the season, even by reversing the line on the reel and using the back taper. There may be nylon floaters with improved dressing whose stretch matches that of the nylon itself, but if so I have not yet come across one.

The dacron lines also have a very smooth finish and are supple and pleasant to use—possibly too supple in some instances. They are best for spring and winter fishing, when it is necessary to get the line well down in the water. They need little care, and it would seem they should last forever. I have not tried floating the American dacron lines because the finish is so smooth it seems unlikely that any grease would cling to them. But there is an English line of the same material, called terylene, that can be made to float well by greasing. It will not float as long as a greased silk line, but has the advantage that it can be dried off by drawing it through a cloth and then regreased at the waterside. This is not good practice with a silk line, which soaks up water, since the grease will seal the water into the line and rot it.

This leaves the fly-fisherman with a difficult choice. I have no doubt at all that silk still makes the best line for all purposes; it will do everything really well, and its only disadvantage is that it needs a certain amount of care. The fisherman who is willing to take a little extra trouble cannot do better than buy himself a silk line.

A fisherman who can afford two lines would probably be well satisfied with a dacron line for winter and spring fishing and a nylon floater for summer and fall. But he should face the fact that he will probably have to replace his nylon line from time to time as the dressing cracks away, unless he is prepared to splice on a new front taper.

LINE SIZES AND TAPERS

The next point to consider in lines is their size, which seems complicated but is not. Fly lines are measured by their diameter in thousandths of an inch, each size reflecting a difference of five one-thousandths and being represented by a letter, as shown in the following table:

A	.060 inch	D	.045 inch	G	.030 inch
B	.055 inch	E	.040 inch	H	.025 inch
C	.050 inch	F	.035 inch	I	.022 inch

Sizes larger than A, for the more powerful salmon and salt-water rods, are shown as 2A, 3A, etc.

Fly lines are usually thirty or thirty-five yards long. They can be bought as "level" lines, that is to say with the same diameter throughout their length, but nearly all fly-fishermen use "tapered" lines, which fine down at each end from a fairly heavy level section in the middle. One can cast quite satisfactorily with a level line, but because a fly line has to be rather thick and heavy to get performance out of the rod, the transition to the light leader is too abrupt. Control is less effective, and the line cannot be set down as lightly and smoothly as it should. A young fisherman starting out to fish a wet fly on swift, broken streams will be perfectly happy with a level line, especially if his rod is light enough to permit him to use one of the smaller sizes. But a tapered line is definitely superior for all types of fishing and worth the higher price. It is wiser for the fly-fisherman to economize on his rod, his reel or any other part of his equipment rather than the line.

THE DOUBLE TAPER

Tapered lines are generally said to be of two types, the double taper and the forward or torpedo taper. I should like to consider these as three different types, for reasons I will make clear. The double taper is simply a length or "belly" of heavy line tapering down through a few feet at each end to a fine point. The purpose of the taper at each end is simply to allow the line to be reversed on the reel when the front taper becomes worn or unduly shortened in use, so that in practice one has two lines for the price of one.

Double-tapered lines are extremely pleasant and satisfactory in use, especially for dry-fly fishing. One can cast accurately and well with them, holding a lot of line in the air beyond the rod top if necessary, and the longest cast still leaves heavy line in the left hand. This can be a real advantage when a fish strikes, because light line has a tendency to knot or kink and cannot be freed so readily and surely from the fingers. A good caster can cast a very long way with a double-tapered line, though he may need a slightly heavier, softer and slower rod than he would to get the same distance with a forward taper. Sizes of double-tapered lines are shown by three letters: GBG, HCH, HDH, IEI, for instance, the middle letter in each case representing the diameter of the belly of the line while the outer letters give the diameter of the points.

TORPEDO AND FORWARD TAPERS

The term "torpedo taper," in my opinion, should not be confused with "forward taper," but should be reserved for lines with very short bellies, say twenty-five feet or less. These lines are the prototypes of the forward tapers, but they are not, again in my opinion, useful for general fishing purposes. They permit very long casts to be made, especially when they are spliced to light nylon monafilament, and they facilitate the casting of heavy bass and salt-water lines with comparatively light rods; they are satisfactory for these purposes, but no other. They force a clumsy, violent and tiring style of casting. Practically all the line must be recovered after every cast, leaving the fisherman with coil upon coil of very light line in his hand, or worse still, in a line basket hanging round his neck. While they may be desirable, or even necessary, in fishing some rivers, I do not think the ordinary fly-fisherman should inflict them upon himself.

Forward-tapered lines are another matter altogether. In most instances these are beautifully designed, thoroughly practical fly-fishing lines, possibly the most satisfactory of all for general use. Developed first of all for tournament casting and redesigned for fishing purposes, these lines will get the best performance out of a rod without forcing the fisherman into abnormalities of style or seriously affecting his line handling. A properly designed forward taper should have at least forty-five feet of belly and front taper before it starts to fine back into the running line. The effect of this is that in casts of ordinary length, especially in dry-fly fishing, one is using a line with most of the virtues of a double taper. To make a long cast, it is necessary only to strip off five or six coils of the lighter "running" line and let it shoot behind the pull of the belly line.

The principle of the double-taper line is to provide

through the whole length of line to be cast the weight necessary to bring out the driving force of the rod and to overcome air resistance; the front taper allows the line to be laid delicately on the water near the fish; a moderate shoot of line from the left hand is readily made at the end of the forward cast, but the thickness of the line slows and limits this.

The principle of the torpedo taper or shooting head is to concentrate the effective line weight into as short a length as possible, usually about twenty feet, so that a short cast brings out the maximum power of the rod, developing a high velocity in the forward drive and permitting an extremely long shoot of the light back taper.

The well-designed forward-taper line combines these two principles by spreading the weighted portion of the line over sufficient length to allow a cast of good average distance (say forty feet) to be carried in the air beyond the rod top, and backing it from there with light line that will shoot readily. Properly matched to a stiffish rod of quick action, the forward taper allows for plenty of velocity and gives the flat, narrow loop in the forward drive of the line that makes for distance. Yet the belly diameter of the line need be no larger than that of a double taper for the same rod, so none of the delicacy and control are lost in presenting the fly to a fish. Forward-taper lines usually have a running line at least one size heavier than the point of the forward taper, so their sizes are expressed by three different letters—GAF, GBF, HCF, HDG and IEH are the usual run of sizes for single-handed rods.

FITTING THE LINE TO THE ROD

Close matching of the line to the rod is extremely important. Too heavy a line overburdens the rod's action, dragging it back and forth in a way that feels top-heavy and uncomfortable; the rod simply cannot develop enough velocity in the line to make casting effective. Too light a line frustrates the power of the rod simply because it cannot flex it sufficiently to bring on any real drive.

There is probably one size and weight of line, and one only, that will get the maximum of power and efficiency out of any given rod, but I do not think this doctrine should be carried too far; there is a sort of safety factor on either side of this ideal that permits a good deal of latitude without significant loss of comfort and efficiency. I have one favorite eight-foot rod, for instance, that is probably at its best with an HDG silk line. But I can use with it, in complete satisfaction, an HCH line of silk or nylon, an HCF terylene and even an IEH dacron and an HEH silk. An HCF dacron sinker proved slightly too heavy for comfort. While I don't recommend such imprecision in selecting a line, I think it is well to realize that there is a certain tolerance.

The sort of rod I have described in Chapter Two, eight and a half feet, four and a half ounces, made of fiber glass and with a stiffish action, should perform satisfactorily with an HCH double-taper or an HCF forward-taper silk line. Theoretically that would mean one size larger or GBG in a nylon floater and one size smaller or HDH in a dacron sinking line, though in practice I have certainly not found this to be so. A line as thick as B, whatever its weight, is likely to prove clumsy and ineffective on an eight-and-a-half-foot rod. The finer HDH sinking line may be an advantage, but only if it proves heavy enough to bring the action out of the rod.

A nine-foot rod of similar character should handle a GBG double taper and a GBF forward taper, while an eight-foot rod would probably be best with HDH and HDG respectively. But these are approximations because of two variables —the individual performance of the fisherman himself and the exact distribution of weight through the working portion of the rod. I have recommended a rod with a "stiffish action" because this is needed to get performance out of a forward-taper line and it is generally the most useful type for all around use. But unfortunately the term "stiffish" is open to a wide range of interpretation—wide enough, certainly, to make the difference of a line size.

Most fly-rod manufacturers suggest the proper line sizes for their rods, either in catalogues or by marking the size on the rod itself, just above the cork handle. This, though it does not allow for the individual variation of the fisherman, is usually a good enough guide. But the ideal way of matching line to rod is to find a friend who owns fly lines of several different sizes and try these out with the rod. If one seems completely satisfactory, as it probably will, it is necessary only to go to the store and buy a line of the same size and material. If none is completely satisfactory, the trials will almost certainly suggest the proper size and weight. Matching lines and rods is a lot of fun and any fisherman can learn a good deal from it—not merely about the right size of line for his rod, but about the mechanics of casting.

BACKING

The thickness of a fly line limits the length that can be fitted on to a reel of satisfactory size and weight, so fly lines are made in fairly short lengths—usually forty yards or less. This more than takes care of casting needs, but it leaves the fisherman short of line if he hooks a heavy fish that decides to run hard.

The usual practice of fly-fishermen has been to "back" their fly lines with much finer lines of considerable strength. Until fairly recently raw silk lines were best for this, since they had great strength, small diameter and good lasting qualities. I now prefer nylon cuttyhunk in nine-, twelve- or fifteen-pound strength, since it is very reasonably priced and will last indefinitely. Fifty yards of backing is enough for most trout waters, but it is just as well to put on a hundred yards if the reel will take it without crowding the fly line.

THE NEW FLY-LINE SIZES

For several years now various new systems of measuring fly lines have been under consideration. With the development of new materials and new methods of line building and line dressing the simple diameter measurement of the old scale no longer necessarily gives an accurate impression of the *weight* of the line, which is the factor that actually gets the work out of the rod. The American Fishing Tackle Manufacturers Association has decided that this difficulty can be overcome by assigning line sizes from No. 1 to No. 12 based on the weight of the first thirty feet of line (exclusive of the taper tip) in grains. The scale necessarily allows for certain manufacturing tolerances and is shown as follows:

SIZE	WEIGHT	RANGE	SIZE	WEIGHT	RANGE
# 1	60 gr.	54–66 gr.	# 7	185 gr.	177–193 gr.
# 2	80	74–86	# 8	210	202–218
# 3	100	94–106	# 9	240	220–250
# 4	120	114–126	#10	280	270–290
# 5	140	134–146	#11	330	318–342
# 6	160	152–168	#12	380	368–392

This scale was officially adopted on January 1, 1962, and is now appearing in tackle catalogues side by side with the old letter system, so that veteran fly-fishers can get used to it by degrees. The line is further described by the letters DT for "double taper" and WF for "weight forward" or forward taper in front of the number, and the letters F, S or I, for "floating," "sinking" or "intermediate" following. The effect of this is that one will match the line to the rod by its number alone, using the letters merely as a guide in choosing the type of line. The old silk double-taper HCH line, it appears, is now rated No. 7 and expressed as follows: DT7I. Should the fisherman want a floating double taper for the same rod he would buy one marked DT7F, which would in fact have a diameter approaching that of the old GBG. Should he want a sinking line with a forward taper he would look for WF7S. This line, then, a size No. 7 in all its possible variations, should be the line that will fit our hypothetical eight-and-a-half-foot glass rod, weighing four and a half ounces.

Whether or not this new system will find favor among fishermen, it is difficult to say. I am inclined to think it will because it is a genuine simplification and it should be right far more often than not. The old difficulty of the variation between individual fishermen and individual casting styles will remain—the assumed thirty feet of line beyond the rod top will not suit all fishermen under all conditions, nor even the same fisherman under widely differing conditions. It is a pity that point sizes will no longer be shown, though some manufacturers are so careless about these that I have found so-called "H" points to be as heavy as .040, or three full sizes larger than their rating, so perhaps the loss is small.

The most serious difficulty may well be in telling one's own lines apart. I usually have half a dozen or so of assorted sizes hanging in coils and another three or four on reels, and often forget which is which. It is a simple matter now to check them with a micrometer. Measuring off thirty feet (excluding the taper tip) and weighing it (in grains) seems a much more complicated process. The obvious solution is to mark all one's lines and keep them marked, but I wonder how many of us will do so.

These, of course, are the mumblings of an old conservative who never found very much difficulty with the old system. There can be no doubt that a new day has dawned and that it is a better day. But I may be forgiven for hoping that the line manufacturers will long continue to show both the old and the new sizes of their lines. And I wish all old fly-fishermen an easy transition and all new ones a ready comprehension.

CHAPTER FOUR

Leaders and Hooks

WHATEVER MAY BE the doubts about the best way of measuring fly lines, there is no doubt among responsible manufacturers and there should be none among fly-fishers that the best way to measure leaders is by diameter, again in thousandths of an inch. This was true in the days of silkworm gut, when the breaking strain of leaders was variable and everyone knew it. It is still true in the day of nylon leaders because different manufacturers claim different, and often extravagant, breaking strains for the same diameter of nylon. The fly-fisherman is much more interested in the diameter (and so the relative visibility) of the leader he is showing his fish than he is in its claimed breaking strain.

If I seem to have summarily dismissed silkworm gut as a leader material, I should like to say that I do so only through force of circumstances. Silkworm gut casts much better than nylon and I believe it is less visible to the fish than nylon of equal diameter, two very important advantages. But its disadvantages weigh heavily against it. It comes only in short lengths, which must be knotted together to make a leader of acceptable length. It must be soaked before using, which is a considerable inconvenience. It cannot be trusted after a season or two, though it may remain good for years. It has become very hard to get. And it is expensive— at least twice, if not three times, as expensive as nylon. Within a very few years it will probably be all but unprocurable at any price. For all these reasons I feel that the modern fly-fisherman may as well forget about silkworm gut and take nylon leaders to his heart.

A fly-fisherman's leader should, like his line, be tapered, and for much the same reasons. He needs a thick butt to his leader so that the transition from the fly line will be smooth and the leader will cast out beyond it, and a fine point so that it will not disturb the fish. The proper diameter for the butt of the leader is controlled by the diameter of the point of the fly line: the standard rule is that the butt or loop end of the leader should be not less than two-thirds the diameter of the point of the fly line, which means, for instance, that with an H point on the fly line (.025″) the butt of the leader should be not less than .017″. In my opinion .019″ is better, especially on a leader longer than nine feet. The point diameter is controlled by the sophistication of the fish and the size of the fly, a combination that calls for further examination. But it is necessary first to list the various leader sizes and their named equivalents. I have shown approximate breaking strains as well, though a true fly-fisherman never concerns himself with these until after he has hooked his fish, and by then it is too late to do anything but use what skill he has.

LEADER SIZES

Size	Diameter	Approx. B/S	Size	Diameter	Approx. B/S
6x	.005″	.75 lb.	9/5	.012″	8 lb.
5x	.006″	1 lb.	8/5	.013″	9.5 lb.
4x	.007″	1.5 lb.	7/5	.014″	11 lb.
3x	.008″	2 lb.	6/5	.015″	13 lb.
2x	.009″	3 lb.	5/5	.016″	15 lb.
1x	.010″	4.5 lb.	4/5	.017″	17 lb.
0x	.011″	6 lb.	3/5	.018″	20 lb.

The breaking strains given in the above table are approximate and probably tend to be too high, though I have tried to strike a rough average for the claims of several manufacturers. The only reason for showing them at all is to offer a rough guide to the fisherman who is used to nylon monafilament, but not to fly leaders. And even he should take warning that while a good length of monofilament line, whatever its nominal breaking strain, is practically unbreakable because of its stretch, a nine-foot leader has very limited stretch and will break much more easily.

The most useful all-around length for leaders is nine feet. Leaders up to fourteen feet are used by some fishermen in waters where fish are particularly shy and leaders of seven and a half feet are convenient with short rods because the fly can then be hooked into the reel fitting without drawing the knot between line and leader through the top guide. These shorter leaders cost a few cents less, but a nine-foot leader permits a fisherman to cut away up to eighteen inches or two feet in the process of tying on new flies and still have a leader of useful fishing length, so the real economy is with the longer length. To overcome the problem of the knot and the top guide when carrying the rod from pool to pool, one simply passes the leader round the reel and hooks the fly into the butt guide.

On the virtues or otherwise of very long leaders I hesitate to pass an opinion. There is a story that an aspiring fisherman once asked the late E. R. Hewitt about them. "I notice, Mr. Hewitt," he said, "that you prefer fourteen-foot leaders. Mr. La Branche generally uses a nine-foot leader."

"Yes," said Hewitt gruffly, "that's why he never catches any fish."

Since both Hewitt and La Branche are securely among the immortals of fly-fishing, one must tread delicately here. Personally I have little doubt that there are particularly exacting places and conditions where leaders twelve or fourteen feet long offer some advantage, but I do not think a fisherman meets with them very often. When he does, he can always lengthen his nine-foot leader by knotting on a few extra feet.

It pays to "fish fine"—that is, to use the lightest leader that fish and fly and water conditions will permit, but it is seldom necessary to use a leader with a point finer than 4x. To some extent, the hook size of the fly must control the size of the leader. Flies tied on No. 18, 20 or smaller hooks practically insist on leaders tapered to 4x or finer, and flies up to 16 fish well and safely on 4x. If he goes beyond 16, to 14 or 12, the fly-fisherman will do well to use a very delicate touch in setting his hook and he would be better with 3x. For flies on hook sizes 10 to 6, 2x is usually fine enough, while 1x and 0x are often not too much, especially in heavy water. For hook sizes larger than 6 and up to No. 2, 9/5 is a good leader size; for No. 1, 8/5 or 7/5 is better and for 2/0 and beyond, 4/5 is really needed, especially under winter conditions.

These are suggestions, of course, rather than absolute rules, but the fly-fisherman must think in terms of matching the size of his leader to the size of his fly rather than of matching it to the size of fish he expects to catch. Merely casting a big fly overstrains a very light leader and setting a big hook into a solid fish with it can be little better than a matter of luck. Yet when the two are properly matched, small flies and fine leaders can be extremely effective; it is probably easier to land a five-pound trout on a 4x leader with a No. 18 fly than on 3x with a No. 6.

Size of leader and size of fly necessarily depend on where, how and for what one is fishing. But the most commonly used leader sizes for trout are probably 1x, 2x and 3x. It is usually wise to carry at least one heavier leader, perhaps tapered to 9/5, and one really light leader as well unless one is very sure of the conditions that will be met.

There is, I believe, some point to staining leaders, especially those made of nylon; skin divers tell me that monafilament shows up like rope in the water. The only convincing experiment I have read of on this matter concerned mullet, a very shy fish, in shallow sandy sloughs in Australia; a red or pink stain was definitely superior to all others. For some years Hewitt's "semi-invisible" stained gut leaders were very popular and I think may have had some advantages; certainly I used them with every satisfaction. This was a dark brown stain, and I have used a similar stain (called root brown) on nylon leaders with equal satisfaction. But I cannot conscientiously claim that this or any other stain makes a significant difference and I do not feel at a disadvantage when using unstained leaders.

FLY HOOKS

Fly hooks are made in a great variety of shapes and sizes for all varieties of fish and fishing. Since most fly-fishermen buy ready-made flies rather than bare hooks, it is not necessary to go very thoroughly into the subject here. But some knowledge of the standard hook scale is pretty well essential to the fly-fisherman and he should also have some idea of the possible variations from the standard.

All good fly hooks have either a downturned or upturned eye—that is, an eye set at an angle to the shank of the hook so that the leader can be passed through it and knotted securely around the shank behind the eye. This provides for a strong hold, and at the same time brings the pull of the leader directly into line with the hook shank. Upturned eyes are more commonly used for dry flies, downturned for wet flies, whose softer hackles do not interfere with the knot.

Standard hook sizes represent the length of the shank (without the eye) to a point level with the outside of the bend of the hook, measured in fractions of an inch. A No. 20 standard hook is $5/32''$ and sizes increase from 20 to 14 by thirty-seconds; from size 14 to size 4 they increase by sixteenths; from there on they increase by eighths of an inch. Hook sizes larger than No. 1, which is $1\frac{1}{4}$, are shown as $1/0$, $2/0$, etc., in an ascending scale. There is also a standard wire diameter for each size of hook, and less precisely, a standard gap between shank and point. The following scale gives the sizes most commonly used by fly-fishermen:

Size No.	Length	Wire Dia.	Size No.	Length	Wire Dia.
2/0	$1\frac{5}{8}''$	.045″	9	$\frac{11}{16}''$	.027″
1/0	$1\frac{1}{2}''$	.043″	10	$\frac{9}{16}''$	.024″
1½	$1\frac{3}{8}''$	.041″	12	$\frac{7}{16}''$	.021″
1	$1\frac{1}{4}''$	.039″	14	$\frac{11}{32}''$	.018″
2	$1\frac{1}{8}''$	.037″	16	$\frac{9}{32}''$	.016″
4	$1\frac{5}{16}''$	.033″	18	$\frac{7}{32}''$	.014″
6	$1\frac{3}{16}''$	.030″	20	$\frac{5}{32}''$	.012″

Variations from the standard are made for special purposes. Streamer hooks, for instance, for long slender flies that usually represent small fish, are shown as 2x long or 3x long—that is, two sizes or three sizes longer than the standard shank length. Heavy hooks, which help to get the fly well down, are shown in the same way, as 2x stout, 3x stout, etc.—that is, two or three sizes heavier than the standard wire diameter. Light hooks, for dry-fly fishing, are 2x fine or 3x fine.

So far as I know, there are no present plans afoot to change any of this. When I began fly-fishing, more than forty years ago, there was a series of "new numbers," beginning at 000 for a No. 18 and going up from there through 00, 0, 1, etc., which was commonly used for dry flies in England. These numbers were printed alongside the standard numbers in the catalogues and will be found in some of the very best books that have been written about fly-fishing—books by Frederic M. Halford, J. W. Hills, G. E. M. Skues, Eric Taverner and many others—which is the only reason I mention them.

CHAPTER FIVE

Flies

THE FIRST important thing to realize about artificial flies for all types of fishing is that there are far too many patterns. The possible combinations of fur, feathers, hair, silver, tinsel, wool and other materials in all their assorted colors are infinite. Thousands, if not tens of thousands, of these combinations have been made up into artificial flies, most of them have had some sort of success at one time or another and a high proportion of them have been given names and a permanent record somewhere. Fly patterns have their importance, but it can be greatly over-emphasized, and the wise fisherman tends to limit his range of choice. The *type* of fly and how and where it is fished will always be of far greater importance than the exact pattern.

There are two, and only two, main types of fly, the wet and the dry. The first is designed to fish somewhere below the surface of the water, the second on the surface. Within each group there are a number of lesser types, most of them of considerable importance, but it is well to establish these two great groupings and their essential differences first. Pattern has nothing at all to do with it; the same pattern may be tied as a dry fly or a wet fly and both will fish to good effect. Though there is no particular point in it, one can in fact fish a wet fly on the surface or a dry fly below it and take fish with both.

The dry fly, being intended to float, is usually rather bushier than the wet, with more bulk in proportion to the size of its hook. It usually has hard, stiff hackles tied to stand out at right angles to the hook shank, while the wet fly has softer hackles tied so that they lie back along the hook shank. Dry-fly wings are usually, though not always, set upright, straight out or pointing forward on the hook, while the typical wet-fly wing is tied to lie backward along the shank. The general appearance of the wet fly is slender and stream-lined; dropped on a table, it lies flat on its side, while the typical dry fly stands up on its hackles.

Dry flies are tied on light hooks, for buoyancy, and are usually oiled or greased before using. Wet flies may be tied on light or heavy hooks, depending on their type and pur-

pose, but are usually on standard hooks. It is a fair generalization that wet flies should not be too heavily dressed in
body or wing or hackle, so that they will sink promptly and
have plenty of action in the water, but there are exceptions
to this also.

DRY-FLY TYPES

It is not entirely easy to separate either dry flies or wet
flies into their various categories or to decide which of these
are significant enough to need definition here. Perhaps the
important point is to emphasize that there are many different ways of tying flies and that, in at least some instances,
these serve different purposes and different styles of fishing.

The standard or orthodox dry fly is, I suppose, the *upright-winged* type, originally tied to represent a floating
May fly. It usually has a few feather fibers for tail, a body of
wool, silk, seal's fur, hare's ear or other material, stiff bright
hackles standing well out just behind the eye of the hook;
and divided, upright wings of hackle tips or strips cut from
a feather are set among these or just ahead of them. I have
used such flies a great deal and caught hundreds of fish on
them; resting on the water, they are often hard to distinguish
from natural flies floating nearby. Yet I am by no means
certain that the wings themselves serve any useful purpose
except that of enabling the fisherman to see his fly more
clearly. The *hackle* dry fly, tied in almost exactly the same
way but without the wings, seems to be taken just as readily
under most conditions and is likely to float better.

Fan-wing and *spent-wing* flies are further variations of
the standard dry fly. The fan-wing has wide, upright wings

FLY TYPES

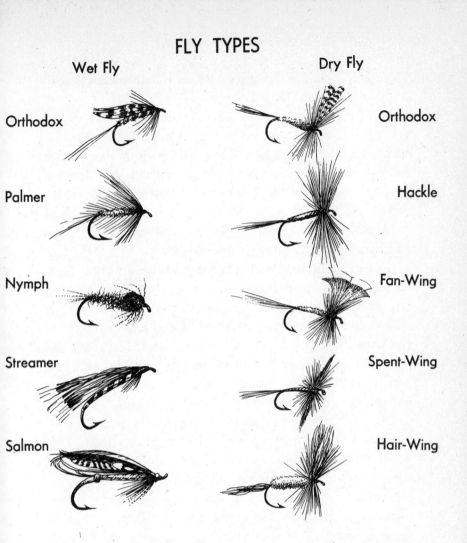

Wet Fly   Dry Fly

Orthodox   Orthodox

Palmer   Hackle

Nymph   Fan-Wing

Streamer   Spent-Wing

Salmon   Hair-Wing

that curve outward; well tied, it is a very beautiful fly. The spent-wing represents the fly exhausted after its breeding flight. It is more sparsely hackled than an upright-winged fly so that it will settle farther into the surface film of the

51

water, like a dead or dying creature, and the wings are spread horizontally from the hook.

Spiders and *variants* are among the most useful of dry flies. The distinction between them is not always clear, but variants are often tied with wings, always with tails and have rather shorter hackles than spiders, though still long in proportion to the hook. They sit high and delicately on the water, are usually floated over the fish without artificial movement and their patterns are impressionistic rather than attempts to imitate some specific insect.

Spiders are dressed with very long hackles, always without wings, often without tails and invariably on small hooks— size 12 is probably too large, sizes 14 and 16 are normal. A spider can be effectively skated or skipped on the surface of the water. Used with a light leader on a breezy day, and nylon is an advantage here, it can be lifted and dropped back with an extremely lifelike effect. Fish that will stir for nothing else are often tempted by spiders or variants.

Dry flies with wings and tail made of hair instead of feathers float extremely well and also take fish well. They are popular for Atlantic salmon and for trout and steelhead on the rougher western streams, but there is really no limit to their usefulness when properly tied in the right sizes to meet local conditions. The wings may be divided and tied at an angle forward, as in the Wulff type, divided and tied upright, or laid back along the hook. Dry-fly wings laid back along the hook, whether of hair or feather, usually represent stone flies or sedges.

WET-FLY TYPES

Wet flies, like dry flies, may be tied with or without wings, but wet-fly wings, whether of hair or feather, serve more than one useful purpose. Being set backwards, along the shank of the hook, they help the fly to swim or drift properly in the water; they give bulk and substance to its silhouette; and they give it lifelike action, either by stirring to the current or in response to the movement of rod and line.

Two simple strips of feather, set on back to back, or several strands of hair, make the usual wet-fly wing. Effective wet flies can also be made by twisting a few turns of soft hackle at the front of the body, just behind the eye of the hook. Still another type, with or without wings, is made by winding the hackle in several turns up along the body and tying it off at the head. This is called *"palmer tying"* and is used in both wet and dry flies, though the hackles should be soft in wet flies, stiff in dry flies.

Some wet flies are made in more or less realistic imitation of May fly, stone fly and caddis *nymphs* or other underwater creatures. These are without wings and have only short, sparse hackles that represent legs and feet. Properly tied of feathers, hair, wool, seal's fur and other standard materials, they can be very effective. The molded rubber and plastic nymphs that look so realistic in the tackle stores are, in my experience, almost useless.

Streamer flies are usually tied on long-shanked hooks to give the appearance of small fish. They are likely to have bright bodies, often of silver tinsel, and bright flexible wings of hair on feathers running the full length of the hook shank and sometimes beyond it. The general effect is that of a large fly or lure which is light enough to be cast by the ordinary fly rod and under some conditions they are certainly very useful, often taking big fish. Though I use them at times, I am never fully satisfied that they are superior to flies dressed in a similar way on standard hooks, as the long hook seems to stiffen and limit their action in the water. The one time I have found them really superior to other flies was when fishing for landlocked Atlantic salmon in Argentina.

Another long-hook type is the *woolly worm*, representing a drowned caterpillar or other largish land creature. It is usually tied with a thick, rough body of wool or chenille, with a hackle wound palmerwise along the body. It is best fished deep and without artificial movement, simply drifting with the current except in recovery.

Atlantic salmon wet flies are not essentially different from ordinary wet flies except in the extreme complication of their patterns. This is chiefly a matter of tradition and aesthetics; full-dressed salmon flies are very handsome and they are certainly attractive to both salmon and trout. But simpler flies of similar size and coloring are probably just as effective and the modern tendency is, on the whole, to simplify. Western *steelhead flies*, usually made with simple hair wings, are a good example of this, and a number of Atlantic salmon patterns always have been made with simple strip wings.

Perhaps the greatest simplification of all is in the *greased-line flies* that are used for Atlantic salmon. These are tied on long, slender hooks, with body and wing covering only the forward part of the hook shank. They are designed to offer a minimum of resistance to the water and are fished just under the surface film, without artificial movement. Greased-line techniques are important in trout as well as salmon fishing, especially under difficult conditions.

Bass flies take many forms. They may be streamers or ordinary wet flies (usually with rather bulky wings), they may be floaters with cork bodies designed to make eccentric movement and even a popping sound when drawn against the water, or they may be designed to dart and wobble under water. All these types can be made light enough to be cast with ordinary fly-fishing gear, though stiffer rods and heavier lines are generally used to give better control.

Spinner flies, heavily *weighted flies* and all flies too heavy to be cast by a singlehanded fly rod are beyond the purpose of this book. Spinner flies are particularly objectionable in that they twist up the line and leader and there is no means of counteracting this without increasing their excessive weight still further.

FLY PATTERNS

A fly "pattern" is simply a certain arrangement of feathers and other materials on a hook. Some patterns call for a certain limited range of hook sizes and many specify the way the materials should be tied in to make the finished fly. But, in theory at least, any "pattern" can be tied to any "type." The famous Royal Coachman, for instance originally a strip-wing wet fly, is now tied either wet or dry, and may be fan-wing, spent-wing, hair-wing wet or dry, Wulff type or variant. Without its white wings I suppose it would no longer be a Royal Coachman, and I do not recall having seen it tied as a greased-line fly, though it would fit the purpose nicely.

I have suggested that named patterns are far too numerous for even the most experienced fly-fisherman to find his way among them all. Fortunately it is entirely unnecessary to do so. Half a dozen patterns are probably enough for most types of fishing and the most useful half dozen are likely to be the local favorites. This makes a logical start, and no doubt it would make a logical end as well, but it never is the end. No fly-fisherman can resist buying new patterns, or resist tying them if he makes his own fles; even if he tries to be strong-minded he will find himself acquiring new patterns by gift or exchange or, it sometimes seems, out of the thin air. So we nearly all end up with boxes and boxes of assorted creations and, what is worse, we usually go out on the stream with five or ten times as many patterns as we are ever likely to need or use.

It is important to buy flies of good quality, which means at least twenty-five cents a piece today and up to fifty or seventy-five cents for larger sizes. Full-dressed Atlantic salmon flies in the standard sizes run well over a dollar. In dry flies look especially for bright, sharp-pointed hackles; in most wet flies look for neat, slim dressing, small heads and good feathers. Have nothing to do with plastic wings or cheeks or sides. They make the fly spin in the air and usually break off very quickly. Cheap flies mean cheap, lusterless materials, poor hooks, inaccurate patterns and, all too often, workmanship that falls to pieces after brief use.

The great assortment of patterns and knowing some of their names and something about them is part of the pleas-

ure of fly-fishing, and there *are* times when the fish seem
to disregard everything except one special pattern that may
or may not be in the box. I have no wish to restrain anyone
from the pleasure of knowledge or the rarer pleasure of
finding the infallible. But one has to start somewhere, and
I feel bound to name two groups of half a dozen patterns
that I think would serve a starting fly-fisherman fairly well
on almost any water. I have limited myself to patterns with
well-known names that should be in almost any good tackle
shop. Hook sizes should be according to local advice. For
wet-fly fishing, the following:

Royal Coachman	(a bright fly)
Black Gnat	(a dark fly)
Professor	(a general fly)
Teal and Silver	(a minnow fly)
Western Bee	(summer and fall)
March Brown	(spring)

And to these add a streamer fly, such as the Muddler Minnow, the Grey Ghost or the Mickey Finn, for good measure.

Dry flies are perhaps more difficult, but I think a fisherman
would be able to get results almost anywhere with the following:

Black Gnat	Red Variant
Brown-and-White Bi-visible	Ginger Spider
Western Bee (or similar pattern)	Quill Gordon or Blue Variant

Add at least one hair fly, such as the Humpy, the Grey Wulff
or the Irresistible.

The next thing is to go out fishing with one or other of
these selections, or perhaps both of them. Ask a fly-fishing

friend to look them over and say which he thinks will do to start with. He will look them over very solemnly and carefully and in the end will shake his head sadly. Then he will reach into his own fly book and hand you something else. "Here," he will say, "you better take this. Those others might be O.K. sometimes. But not here, not today." The six, already seven, have now become eight.

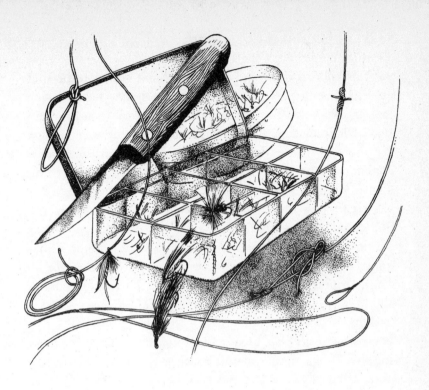

CHAPTER SIX

Knots and Paraphernalia

WE NOW HAVE the fly-fisherman's essentials—
rod, reel, line, leader and flies. The next point is
to put them all together so they will work properly. For this one needs three or four knots and two splices,
neither of which is properly a splice. The simplest thing is
to work from the reel outwards and examine them one by
one.

Backing to reel. No fly-fisherman really expects ever to

put this knot to a test and some few don't bother to tie it at all. As a result, it occasionally happens that fish, backing and an expensive fly line are all lost in one agonizing second of helplessness. Any time the last few turns of backing are showing on the drum of the reel the wise fisherman is running his hardest, or perhaps swimming if the circumstances so dictate. At such times, rare though they may be, it is well to have the knot there. What sort of a knot doesn't matter too much so long as it is solid. I pass the end of the backing around the drum and tie it in some sort of a slip-knot (a bowline or a clove hitch or two half-hitches are all fine) around the long end, then pull the resulting noose tight on the drum. After that, simply reel on the rest of the backing.

Backing to fly line. One can buy fly lines whipped to backing, but it is a simple matter to do it oneself. Fray out the ends of the fly line and the backing, wax them well, then whip them firmly together with close turns of fine, waxed silk or nylon thread. Roll in two or three coats of clear nail polish between finger and thumb to protect the whipping. This makes a smooth, neat, tapered join that will pass readily back and forth through the rings of the rod, but it limits the backing to use with a single fly line unless one is willing to repeat the whole process at every change. A better method is to fray out the end of the backing, wax it and bring it back on itself in a loop wide enough to pass the reel through, then whip it with silk or nylon. Do the same thing with the back end of the fly line, except that this loop can be a very small one. Then pass the backing loop through the fly-line loop, bring it back over the reel and let the two loops pull firmly together. This connection will not pass quite so smoothly through the rings of the rod, but the important advantage is that one can change from one fly line to another in the matter of a minute or two. One reel and one length of backing can serve several lines of different qualities. The change from a floating to a sinking line could even be made at the waterside if one chose, though most fishermen prefer to carry two reels or a spare drum for this.

Fly line to leader. A second small loop can be whipped into the front end of the fly line; the loop of the leader is passed through this and the end of the leader through its own loop. Then the loops of line and leader can be tightened together exactly as those of the backing and fly line. There is nothing against this method except that the end of the fly line sometimes gets cracked and worn so that the loop

TUCKED SHEET BEND

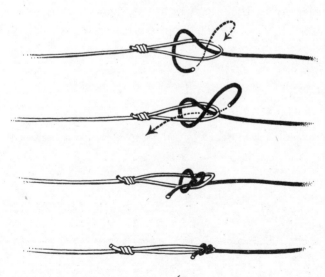

must be cut off and made again. I think I prefer on the whole to tie on the leader with the well-known figure-eight knot or with a tucked sheet bend. Both knots are started in the same way, by passing the end of the line through the loop of the leader, bringing it around and under itself (that is, between the line and the leader loop). The tuck is made by pushing the short end of the line through its own bend and pulling the line tight on the leader loop. The figure-eight knot is made by passing the short end of line round the standing line, which makes a clear eight, and then passing it through both loops of the eight. This knot is pulled down on the leader loop in the same way, holding the short end between the thumbnail and first finger of the left hand. The figure eight is probably the more secure of the two, but the tucked sheet bend is freed more easily when the time comes to change leaders.

Point to leader. Some fly-fishermen like to preserve or control the size of their leaders by tying in an extra point, about eighteen inches long, from time to time as the old

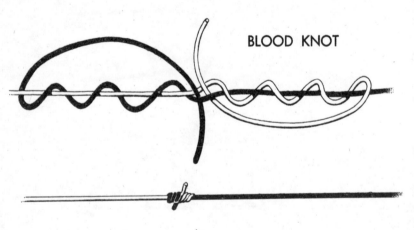

BLOOD KNOT

point is cut off in tying on new flies. Others like to make up their own tapered leaders by tying together short lengths of nylon of different thickness. For either of these purposes a double blood knot or else a double fisherman's knot is fine. The double blood is the better of these two, though the double fisherman is easier to tie. To tie a double blood, overlap the two strands by two or three inches. Twist the right-hand strand two or three times around the left, bring the end back and pass it between the two strands. Then, holding this short end securely between thumb and forefinger of the left hand, twist the left-hand strand two or three times around the left, bring the end back and pass it between the two strands in the opposite direction to the other one. Now tighten the two knots against each other by pulling on the long ends of the strands. The effect should be a neat knot of four or six firm coils, with the two short ends standing out at right angles between them. Clip off these short ends close against the knot.

The double fisherman achieves much the same effect. The start is the same, overlapping the two ends. Bring the right strand around the left in two or three loose overhand loops,

DOUBLE TURLE

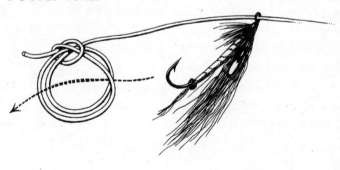

63

bring the short end back and then forward again through these loops and pull the resulting knot tightly down on the left-hand strand. Repeat the process in the opposite direction and then slide the two knots until they meet by pulling gently but firmly on the strands. The advantage is that one end of the knot is finished before the other, which makes tying easier. The disadvantages are that the knot is a little bulkier, since it encloses two strands instead of one, and the short ends lie parallel with the leader and so cannot be trimmed quite so tidily. I have not known either knot to slip when properly tied.

Fly to leader. The synthetics, and nylon especially because of its stretch, are all more difficult to knot securely than silk or silkworm gut. The figure eight is an excellent knot for tying a fly to a gut leader, giving two firm loops around the hook shank immediately behind the eye and a short end that lies tidily parallel with the hook shank. With nylon it is not trustworthy; nor, I think, is the single turle except possibly with fine leaders and very small flies. By far the best knot I have found for nylon and flies of all sizes is the double turle. Pass the point of the leader through the eye of the fly and push the fly up out of the way. Make two complete loops at the point of the leader, each about an inch in diameter and lying one on top of the other. Tie them together with a simple overhand knot and pull this tight, leaving about a quarter of an inch of the leader beyond it. Bring the fly down, pass it completely through the two loops and bring the eye against the knot. Tighten slowly by pulling on the leader so that the first loop, then the second, closes gently down on the shank of the hook immediately behind the eye. With dry flies especially, care must be taken to keep the loops from catching up the hackles and spoiling the shape of the fly. Thumb and forefinger of the left hand again do most of this.

In tightening all nylon knots, it is important to remember to slide the hand a foot, or preferably more, up the leader from the knot before applying the tightening strain. If the strain is applied close to the knot the result is nearly always a permanent curl in the leader. Never undo and retie a nylon knot. The material fatigues easily and is likely to be much weakened. For the same reason it is wise to cut off the fly and tie it on again after playing a heavy fish or even after casting for some while without hooking a fish; this is particularly important in winter fishing, when temperatures are low, or when using a fly with a big hook.

Splicing fly line. Occasionally a good fly line is accidentally cut or bruised in some way. The damaged part can be cut out and the line rejoined. Sometimes the fisherman wants to splice on a new front taper to an old line or a different running line to his forward taper. A few fishermen like to make up their own lines by splicing together short lengths of line of different diameter. One splice will serve all these purposes. Fray out about a quarter inch of the ends of the two lines to be spliced—a big darning needle is probably the best instrument for this—divide the frayed ends into two equal parts and wax them well. This makes two forks or Y's that can be fitted into each other. The frayed ends should be carefully tapered down with a pair of sharp scissors, the whole of the join firmly whipped with fine waxed thread and finished off by rubbing in some lacquer. It is quite easy to make this splice, but it is very important to finish it smoothly and carefully so that it will slide easily through the rings of the rod in casting.

The ideal way to go fly-fishing is with rod, reel and line, a couple of spare leaders and a few flies in a box. Most of us start out this way in our youth when wading in old pants and bare feet or a pair of worn hobnailed boots comes naturally. But age, sophistication and rheumatism creep up on us and with them comes a complicated array of supplementary gear that can only be called paraphernalia or, more briefly, junk. We should be better off without most of it, but some of it offers conveniences which, in time, we cannot do without.

Waders and Special Clothing. In most parts of North America the fly-fisherman has to wade to get at his streams properly. Hip waders are satisfactory on small streams of fairly even depth, but on larger streams they are the surest way of getting wet I know. One is always tempted to use them to the limit and then a slip, a moment's forgetfulness or an unexpected surge of current means boots full of water. Some fishermen are naturally cautious and make sure they always have a few inches to spare; others carry a pair of dry socks and take their chances. But the best solution is a pair of breast waders. One may never want to wade more than a few inches deeper than one would with hip waders, but it is an important few inches and there is an ample safety factor above and beyond them.

The modern boot-foot wader, with ankle boots of rubber fused to fabric uppers, is fairly expensive—usually around thirty dollars—but it is the most satisfactory wader I know. With reasonable care a pair should last several seasons.

They are easy to put on and take off and not too bulky to pack. Stocking-foot waders of fair to good quality are considerably cheaper to buy, but wading shoes of some sort are necessary and heavy wool socks must be worn between the shoe and the wader to limit abrasion by sand and gravel. All this adds up to a considerable nuisance value and the economy is somewhat doubtful, as stocking-foot waders rarely wear well. I have not had any experience with plastic boot-foot waders, but these can be found at fifteen dollars or less and would seem a better buy.

In streams with bottoms of sand or small gravel, rubber-soled waders are satisfactory. But where the bottom is rocky or made up of round boulders, felt soles are essential. On slab rock soft metal nails or cleats are safer than felt. Some boot-foot waders are made with felt soles and these are fine, though more expensive than they should be. The felt soles wear out long before the waders and it is not, in my experience, at all easy to replace them. I no longer try to. Instead I buy felt-soled sandals made in Boulder, Colorado; these cost about ten dollars a pair and fit on right over the boots. While somewhat heavier, they last considerably longer than the original felts and I am inclined to think that the wise thing is to buy rubber-soled waders in the first place and use the felt sandals with them from the start. The sandals can be removed when one is not actually wading and felts last longer for that.

A raincoat of some kind is essential for a fly-fisherman. For boat fishing it should be long and full-skirted. For wading it should be short and light. None of these requirements presents any special difficulty today; modern raincoats made of nylon and other synthetics are available in every conceivable shape and style. They do keep out rain and it is easy to find a good one that rolls up into little more than a fistful and weighs practically nothing at all.

A fishing vest is not an essential, but I have found them far more convenient and comfortable than creels or bags. They are light and cool, have pockets for everything, can be worn outside the waders or tucked into the top of them if one is wading deeply. There are several different types, including some that double as inflatable life vests, and all are good.

Containers. Fly boxes are no longer a problem. There is nothing better than the modern transparent plastic box, for wet flies or dry. I prefer a box of about four inches by seven inches, with rounded corners and ten or more compartments. If one is using large dry flies it is important to see that the compartments are large enough to hold them without crushing wings or hackles. Leader boxes are no longer important unless one is using silkworm gut; then it is desirable to have a flat box with two flat pads to soak a spare leader in glycerin or water. For nylon leaders, there are neat boxes with transparent envelopes that are a pleasant convenience, but really anything will do or they can be carried loose in their own envelopes.

Gadgets. Perhaps I should not include nets and gaffs under this heading. There are places where they are essential and a net is always useful for carrying fish. I dislike using a gaff and never do so if I can help it, though I usually carry one for winter steelhead. The most useful type for stream use is English or Scottish made and has a telescopic handle of triangular steel.

There is no such thing as a satisfactory net except when one is fishing from clear and open banks or a boat. There a good big net with a long handle that folds in half on a knuckle joint is just fine and probably necessary. When one is wading or traveling brushy banks, as is nearly always the case, all nets get in the way and anything large enough to be of real use is a persistent nuisance. Yet it is only on streams that have unlimited sand and gravel bars that one can safely dispense with a net, and even here there may be spots where a net makes the difference between landing and losing a large fish. Perhaps the least offensive net is the one with two folding arms that extend into a triangle, and in its most useful form this also has a telescopic handle. Another useful type folds back on the handle of a wading staff. Short-handled nets that do not fold are awkward to carry except over the back and even here they catch brush. Avoid the elastic cords that go with these last. The net may catch up in traveling, the cord extends if one isn't watching and the net may come free at the wrong moment with something approaching lethal force. A friend assures me that he was knocked punchy for a whole afternoon in this way; he jumped off a big log, the net caught and tore and the handle hit him squarely behind the ear.

A good sharp knife should be in every man's pocket wherever he goes and a fisherman has special uses for one, such as cleaning fish. In addition a fly-fisherman is wise to carry a pair of nail clippers, fastened somewhere on his person by a short cord; nothing is more useful for clipping off short lengths of leader, trimming fly hackles and other such purposes.

A small pocket thermometer, though certainly not essential, is an instructive gadget and may at times suggest the right places to fish. Most fish are markedly affected by temperature—trout, for instance, are most active and responsive at temperatures from 45° to 60° F.—and a thermometer can help in the discovery of favorable spots, such as the entry of cooler tributary streams, the outlet of cold springs or the layering of temperatures in a lake.

Beyond these every fisherman has a few special things that seem to belong in his equipment. It is well to keep them at a minimum, to check once in a while to be sure that they really do fill some useful purpose. Long ago I learned to ask myself on starting out to go fishing: Rod? Reel? Line? Leaders? Flies? Net? Forget anything else, if you will. With these at least you can fish when you come to the stream.

CHAPTER SEVEN

The Overhead Cast and Others

CASTING is a very important part of a fly-fisherman's skill. Understanding of the ways of water and fish, knowledge and touch in working his fly may be more important, but these skills cannot be put to proper use, nor even acquired, without a reasonable proficiency in casting. Skillful casting is also a considerable part of a fly-fisherman's pleasure. It is in itself a delicate and satisfying art and adequate performance makes all the difference between comfort and discomfort, pleasure and frustration.

Reasonable proficiency in casting a fly is not at all difficult to attain, but it does take a little effort and conscious thought. Thirty minutes of expert instruction is enough to start a beginner out in the way he should go and from that start he can go on improving for years by practice and experience. But without that brief guidance it is possible to wave a rod around almost indefinitely without achieving much more than a set of bad habits and a sense of inadequacy.

THE OVERHEAD CAST

The essential principles of all fly casting are in the simple overhead cast. Once a fisherman has learned the movements and timing of this he can go on to anything else without difficulty.

I have, I hope, already given a clear idea of the importance of the fly line and its weight. The mechanics of fly casting are simply this: the line is thrown back through the air by the impulse of the rod; as it passes the caster's shoulder its weight begins to pull on the rod top; at the moment it straightens out behind the caster the rod is fully flexed, under the maximum desirable tension; at this precise moment the caster exercises the power of this tension by a simple forward movement of hand and wrist and arm; the rod responds, releasing its tension into the forward drive of the line that makes the cast. This is the theory behind the overhead cast that is expressed in the fly-fisherman's axiom: "It must be allowed to straighten out behind if it is to go forward straight."

This theory is not difficult to put into effect; it is simply a

72

matter of timing, and a surprisingly limited amount of practice is enough to develop sufficient accuracy of timing to produce reasonably good and satisfying casts.

The first point to establish is the grip of the hand on the rod. This should be about halfway up the cork handle, absolutely firm and solid, but not tense or rigid. All four fingers are curved round the handle, the little finger, third finger and middle finger contributing most of the firmness by pressing the cork solidly into the fleshy part of the palm, near the heel of the hand. The forefinger supports and steadies this grip but supplies its own firmness against the thumb, which should be along the upper side of the handle and somewhere near the top of the grip. A few casters point the forefinger instead of the thumb along the handle, claiming that greater accuracy and delicacy is obtainable by doing so. But I am satisfied that this is not advisable because it restricts the flexibility of the wrist and materially reduces the firmness and solidity of the grip.

The best place to practice casting and develop timing is on dry land, not out on the water, and a fair-sized lawn is ideal for the purpose. To make a trial cast, put rod and reel down on the grass, draw off about thirty feet of line beyond the rod top and stretch this straight out. Pick up the rod, holding the line against the butt with the forefinger, and throw the line upwards and backwards with a firm, crisp movement that stops the rod in a perpendicular position over the right shoulder. Pause for a moment for the line to straighten out behind, then bring the rod firmly forward to an angle of about twenty degrees from horizontal. The line should come forward and settle out in a straight line along the grass.

It probably will not do so the first time, nor for several times thereafter. The beginning caster almost invariably makes two mistakes: he carries the rod back too far, and he does not wait long enough to let the line straighten out behind him before starting his forward movement. Both of these are crucial because they destroy the timing that develops and uses the tension of the rod. Two other common mistakes are insufficient force in the pickup, or backward movement of the rod, and excessive force in the forward movement. The pickup must be firm and positive, a backward and upward throw of the line that gives it sufficient velocity to straighten out in the air at the level of the rod top. The forward throw calls for slightly less force, since the line is already in the air, but it should still be a firm movement, precisely timed to the full extension of the line behind the caster.

The best and quickest way I know for a beginner to get the feel of these movements and their timing is to allow a skillful caster, standing behind his right shoulder, to make the cast while he himself leaves his hand passively on the rod grip. When this has been done several times the instructor will sense that his pupil is accurately following his movements. A few repetitions, with time in between for trial and error without guidance, should produce a reasonable measure of success.

Failing such expert assistance, a sympathetic friend can do almost as well by watching and telling the caster (a) whether or not he has stopped his backward throw with the rod in a vertical or nearly vertical position and (b) whether the line has fully straightened out before the beginning of the forward movement. It is sometimes a help in checking the backward movement to slip the butt of the rod into the sleeve of the caster. Counting aloud or mentally can help with the timing and the caster himself can glance backwards to check on the movements of rod and line.

SHOOTING LINE

Once the timing and movements of the rod hand are under control, it is time to put the other hand to work. The left hand (I am assuming throughout that the caster is right-handed) is the line hand in fly-fishing. It is used to strip line from the reel, to hold tension on the line through the pickup and backcast and the start of the forward cast, to release line for the "shoot" at the end of the forward cast and to recover line when the cast is fished out. Complete mastery of all this and proper co-ordination with the movements of the rod hand takes a certain amount of time and practice, but a reasonable (and effective) competence is quite easily acquired.

At the beginning of the lift or backcast, the left hand should be holding the line an inch or two beyond the forward end of the rod grip. As the lift is made the left hand should be dropped a little, then allowed to drift upwards towards the rod hand in the backcast, feeling the line and maintaining tension. As the rod starts forward the left hand should be brought down to the left side, at full arm stretch, to ease forward and release the line as the rod is stopped at its forward limit and the cast is completed. If this is properly done, some degree of line pull will be felt against the left hand from beginning to end of the cast; it should be strongest at the pause of the backcast and at the completion of the forward cast.

To shoot line one simply holds two or three loose coils of line in the left hand and releases them at the end of the forward drive of the rod, just as the forward-moving loop of line in the air is exerting its strongest pull. This allows the whole length of line from reel to fly to extend smoothly forward and it is then dropped gently to the water by a slight yielding of the rod top. The effect of shooting line is to add greatly to the distance cast without any great increase of effort, and at the same time to cushion the forward drive of the line so that it remains delicate and controlled.

Once the caster has reached the stage where he can regularly and successfully shoot line and so has extended his casting distance from thirty to forty or forty-five feet, he has mastered the essential principles of all casting. He can go on from there to learn any cast he wants and what is more, he can go out and catch fish. He will not be comfortable or even effective under all conditions, but he is performing like a fly-fisherman and every bit of practice he gets from then on, whether on dry land or on the water, will contribute to his improvement.

Casting a fly cannot be considered an exacting physical performance, but there is no doubt that strength of fingers and hand and wrist play a considerable part. Presumably the best exercise for these particular muscles is casting and more casting. But if this is not possible it may be well to try the old athlete's trick of squeezing and releasing a rubber ball. It should also be emphasized that though wrist and hand play a major part, the whole arm is used quite freely and naturally in casting. There is an ancient theory that the elbow should be kept firmly at the side, so that all movement is limited to the wrist and forearm; some instructors taught their pupils to hold a book between elbow and side while practicing, just as cellists were taught before Casals. This is pure nonsense. The elbow should lift naturally with the rod as the demand comes on the muscles of the upper arm; in making very long casts the whole arm may be extended upwards, adding at least two feet to the length of the rod. Properly controlled, this freedom produces a natural style that is comfortable to the performer and pleasing to anyone who happens to be watching him; and it is inevitably far less tiring to a beginner than anything more restricting.

I hope I have not made this sound difficult, because it is not difficult in practice and once the timing of the line in the air, the wait between the lift and the forward cast while the backcast straightens out behind, has been thoroughly acquired, the rest follows almost naturally. There is also a good deal of scope for individual variation—the movements I have suggested for the left hand, for instance, are probably better acquired by feeling than by positive thought, though it is highly desirable to use the hand to maintain tension on the line throughout the cast. If it does not, loose line slips down through the rings of the rod during the backcast and the power of the rod is largely lost in taking up this slack at the start of the forward cast.

SUPPLEMENTARY CASTS

While the overhead cast is the best of all casts for accuracy, distance and control, it is not enough by itself to make the fisherman comfortable and efficient under all conditions. Comfort and competence are, I believe, the two points a fly-fisherman should strive for in his casting, and by this I mean comfort under all conditions and competence under all conditions. Casting a very long line is not often important; accuracy is important most of the time and so is delicacy. But comfort is important all the time, because it makes the difference between pleasure and misery, and one does not go fishing to be miserable.

By comfort I mean a pleasant sense of co-ordination between rod and line and arm; I mean being able to cast effectively against a stiff wind; I mean being able to get the fly where you want it, under trees and bushes, close against obstructions, and being able to do so in spite of brush and trees and rocky banks that limit or completely frustrate the backcast. The fly-fisherman who spends much time with his fly hung up in trees or his hook broken off by striking against the rocks behind him is not usually a happy man.

This measure of comfort and assurance can only be realized by developing an easy familiarity with several supplementary casts that allows one to counteract the effect of nearly all obstructions. In time, a fisherman will develop many of these on his own, without taking much conscious thought. But it is quicker and better to recognize them and learn them so that they become a part of one's stock in trade, to be drawn on automatically as needed.

One of the most useful, and certainly the easiest to learn of these variations, is the sidearm cast. It is made almost exactly as the overhead except that the left foot and the left side of the body are drawn well around towards the line of the cast and the rod is held and moved horizontally throughout the cast. The line is within a few feet of the water and the fly can be thrown up under bridges or under low-hanging bushes or tree limbs on either bank. In fishing heavily brushed streams the sidearm cast is extremely useful to the right-handed fisherman working upstream along the left bank or downstream along the right bank, since it keeps his line and fly well clear of the overhang.

It is wise, and extremely useful, to be ambidextrous in casting, but few of us are willing to put in the necessary effort to achieve this and most of us end up with a strong preference for one hand or the other. This is only justification for the backhand cast. This is made with the shoulder and right side angled in the direction of the cast, the rod and right hand across the body at about chest height. As in the sidearm, the rod is held more or less horizontally, the line is kept low and the fly comes in low to its target. In both these casts, but in the backhand especially, the wrist and forearm do most of their work; about the only difficulty in learning them is that of getting the necessary muscles used to the work. The backhand serves the right-handed fisherman upstream along the left bank, downstream along the right bank. It follows, of course, that either cast can be varied through ninety degrees from horizontal to the vertical position of the overhead, as conditions dictate.

A cast known as the "steeple" is yet another variation of

the overhead, designed in this instance to clear obstructions behind the caster by keeping the line high on the backcast. The difference is mainly in the pickup, which is made with a strong wrist movement that forces the work into the upper sections of the rod and follows on into a full arm movement. A fairly short line can be thrown up almost vertically by such a pickup and then forced outward by an accurately timed movement of wrist and arm. This is designed to avoid a solid wall of obstruction behind and is not easy, nor really very effective; a roll cast or one of its variations will always do the same thing better. The steeple cast is effective and useful, though, in its more modified forms, which throw line and fly well above the rod top on the backcast, yet bring sufficient tension on the rod to permit a long forward cast and shoot.

The wind cast is yet another variation of the overhead. Its purpose is to force the line directly against a strong wind and it is really a follow-through of power achieved by continuing the forward drive of the rod top beyond the normal point of stop. It is not really a forcing movement at all and excessive force will defeat its purpose. It is best to think of it as a continuing late application of power that brings the rod top almost to the water. It can be learned only by trial and error. A moderate adverse wind should make little difference to the caster if his rod and line are in balance and his timing is accurate. In severe cross winds both sidearm and backhand casts are very useful.

CHAPTER EIGHT

The Roll Cast and Others

ALL THE CASTS SO FAR described assume that the line, leader and fly will have a full travel above or behind the caster on his backcast. The roll cast and its variations keep the line almost entirely in front of him throughout its travel. It is easy to see that this can be an important advantage in fishing heavily brushed streams. There are, in fact, rather few North American trout streams that can be properly fished without roll casting.

81

It is pretty well impossible to learn or practice roll casting on dry land, because much of the effectiveness of the cast depends on the proper use of the tension of the water on the line and fly. The beginning of the roll cast is made by a steady, even lift of the rod that brings the line towards the fisherman and well up to the surface of the water. There is no effort to lift the line itself, but as the rod is brought towards the vertical the weight of the line will form a loop between the rod top and where it enters or rests on the water. The rod is kept moving, somewhat past the vertical position, until the loop is near the right shoulder of the fisherman. At this point it will be exerting some backward tension on the rod top. The rod hand is then lifted rather more quickly to head height and the rod is brought over and down into a forward cast by a firm throw of the wrist. This whole movement, from the first drawing of the line, should be continuous. The effect of the forward cast is to roll the loop over and throw it forward. This in turn draws the front end of the line and the fly swiftly along the top of the water, almost to the feet of the fisherman; at this point, the weight of the line loop, now rolling firmly forward, comes sharply against the tension of the line in the water, picks it up and curves the leader and fly over and beyond itself into the full length of the cast.

Though it may not sound so, this is an easy cast to make. Again, it depends almost entirely on timing and it is important at first not to attempt to roll too much line. Once the timing has been perfected, it is easy enough to roll from thirty to fifty feet and shoot line as well.

The roll cast has many uses. With it the fisherman can

get his line out in many places where trees and brush make the ordinary overhead or sidearm casts impossible. It can be used where there are steep rocky banks or gravel bars behind and the least drop of a backcast will almost certainly lead to a broken hook. It can be used to return the fly quickly to a fish that has missed its strike. It is extremely valuable, too, in recovering line and laying it out on the surface of the water for the pickup of an overhead cast, especially when one is using a sinking line. It is equally good sometimes as the first pickup of a floating line when one is fishing a dry fly upstream. All these, and probably other uses as well, suggest themselves naturally to the fisherman once he has perfected his roll cast and made it a part of his regular performance.

The ordinary roll cast has one considerable disadvantage, especially in stream fishing. It does not readily permit a change of direction in the cast; the line must go out within some twenty or thirty degrees of its point of origin. This is not too unsatisfactory in lake fishing or in fishing a nymph upstream, but for the wet-fly fisherman who is casting almost straight across and allowing his fly to swing around to a point directly below him, it is clumsy and awkward. He must make two or three casts in succession to bring his line around to the point he wants and in doing so he will be disturbing the water quite unnecessarily.

There are two variations of the roll cast that completely overcome this difficulty, the spey cast and the double spey cast. Both were developed on Scottish salmon streams by men using long, limber doublehanded fly rods, but both can be adopted to the uses of the modern fly-fisher with his light singlehanded rod; together, the two of them enable a wet-fly fisherman to work over any stream, no matter how heavily brushed its banks, with a high measure of efficiency and complete comfort.

The spey cast is started with the fly trailing in the current directly downstream of the fisherman and the rod pointing downstream toward it. The fisherman is facing across the stream, in the direction he wants to cast, and he draws the rod, at full arm's length, with a steady sweeping motion across his chest. The effect of this is to bring the fly riffling upstream towards him and to lift it, still a few feet below him, into the air. It passes him, a rod's length in front of him, and as it does so he drops his rod hand so that the fly is pitched to the water on the upstream side of the rod. As it touches the water the fisherman sweeps the rod back over his right shoulder and loops the line out in front of him in a roll cast; the fly will follow and the direction may be controlled almost as one wishes—upstream, straight across or quartering downstream. In other words the direction can be changed as much as a hundred and fifty degrees or so in a single cast.

The advantages of the cast are obvious. It has two disadvantages with a singlehanded rod: the timing is fairly difficult and must be reasonably exact and the abrupt change of direction can overwork the rod if one tries to cast too far. With a glass rod of good quality this probably does not matter, but it is easy to spring the gluing of a cane rod or even to break it at the ferrule. I usually limit myself to forty or fifty feet with an ordinary trout rod, though one can shoot some additional line, especially with a forward taper.

The cast is used by a right-handed fisherman from the left bank or by a left-handed fisherman from the right bank.

The double spey is an altogether easier and smoother cast and so comfortable to use that I often fish it when an overhead would be possible. This is a right-hander's cast from the right bank or vice versa. The start of the cast, again, is with line and fly trailing straight downstream, the rod pointing straight to it and the fisherman more or less squared towards the direction of his cast. The rod is swept upstream at full arm's length, as in the spey, except that the movement is now backhanded. The fly does not leave the water, but riffles upstream until it is directly opposite the fisherman, in fast water, or a little below him in slower water. The rod is raised straight up and circled back, the rod hand passing at face level, then rod and line loop are dropped backward over the right shoulder and the rod is brought round and over for a roll cast in the chosen direction. At this point the fly must be slightly downstream of the axis of the rod's travel, so that it will pickup and loop out without striking the rod. The whole cast is a single, continuous movement, perfectly smooth and quite easy to time and control. One can get good distance without straining the rod and when the timing is right the line shoots well.

Both the spey and the double spey, like the ordinary roll, are useful in bringing a sinking line to the surface before an overhead pickup. But the two speys permit a change of direction at the same time: one simply makes the chosen spey cast with a short line and picks up from that into the overhead. It is a smooth performance, not without considerable grace, and has the important advantage of keeping a wet fly in the water most of the time. Both casts are useful at times in high winds, when one has difficulty in controlling a backcast. And they should not be forgotten when a bank or shoreline is close behind. Nothing is more annoying than rising a good fish and finding that the hook has been broken on a dropped backcast.

There are casts other than these I have described, but these are enough. Anyone who has mastered the overhead, side-arm and backhand, with roll, spey and double spey, will find himself a pretty complete fly-fisherman, able to perform comfortably and efficiently under any conditions he is likely to meet. He will also be able to acquire any other cast that takes his fancy without too much difficulty.

In casting for distance, many modern fly-fishers use what is known as the "double haul" or "double pull." This is a more positive application of keeping the line under tension throughout the overhead cast and it certainly does develop the maximum power of the rod as nothing else can. The first "haul" or "pull" is made with the pickup, speeding the travel of the line through the air; then, as the pull of the back-cast develops, the left hand is drifted up towards the butt ring of the rod, to be brought sharply down again in the second haul or pull as the forward drive begins. With a forward taper and a light running line this permits the caster to shoot a prodigious distance. I am not enthusiastic about this style of casting for several reasons: it is hard work and rather ugly; light running line is difficult to handle; and it encourages a tendency to cast farther than one has to, which is always a mistake in any kind of fishing. But there are some big rivers where no other cast will reach the fish satisfactorily and if I were fishing such a river I have no doubt I would quickly forget my prejudices.

I have not attempted to describe casting with a double-handed rod, because these are seldom used in North America except on a few eastern Atlantic salmon rivers. Double-handed rods are very pleasant to fish with, in spite of their weight and size. It is not difficult for a singlehanded rod man to adapt to them with fair success since most of the casting principles are the same, though the timing is slower and the line handling is different.

Accuracy in casting is just as important as getting the fly out to a reasonable distance. I do not think it can be taught; it is a matter of practice and what teaching is done is done by the fish themselves—a good big fish, rising nicely, scared off by a sloppy cast is a wonderful inducement to do better next time. But here again, dry-land practice can be extremely helpful. The best method I know is to mount rod, reel, line, leader and fly, the last with the hook cut off in line with the shank, and set out a six-inch cereal bowl at a suitable distance. By casting at this and trying to make the fly land in the bowl *and stay there,* one can achieve an advanced degree of both accuracy and delicacy. It is advisable to change the distance quite frequently and to make a point of practicing with, against and across whatever wind there may be. When this becomes too easy, set the bowl under some overhanging limbs or tightly between two bushes. Resist the temptation to slam the fly into the bowl and hope it will stay there. The point is to drop it in gently, exactly as one would drop it on the water in front of a rising fish.

CHAPTER NINE

Wet-Fly Fishing

WET-FLY FISHING may be broadly defined as fishing a fly below the surface film of the water, and this includes everything from the bottom of the stream to the underside of the surface film itself. The surface film of water is something that actually exists. It has a certain tensile strength that will support things having a slightly greater specific gravity than water—the legs of an aquatic fly, for instance, such as a May fly or a sedge, dent it but do not pierce it; it will support most land insects at least briefly, though their drowning struggles tend to break through it and allow them to sink; underwater creatures such as snails and many forms of sedge larvae can cling to the underside of it and travel along it quite effectively, even though they sink abruptly as soon as their hold is broken. It is rather important for a fly-fisherman to know this and to be able to visualize it; it is well to remember, for instance, that his floating line is supported on the surface film, and that more creatures on which fish feed are likely to be found on it or just under it than anywhere else except on the bottom.

Wet-fly fishing is undoubtedly the oldest form of fly-fishing, simply because the weight of any fairly primitive hook is bound to be enough to sink a few untreated feathers tied to it. It was not until some time early in the nineteenth century that anyone seems to have developed the idea of deliberately trying to keep a fly floating by drying it off between casts.

There has been a tendency to discount wet-fly fishing as the lesser art. This will not bear serious examination. To be really good at his business the wet-fly fisherman must understand a number of different techniques; he must be able to control and work his fly effectively at different depths; he must understand something of how fish behave in the water, where they are likely to be resting or feeding; and he must know how to judge these things from the surface of the water unless he already knows his stream very intimately.

THE ORDINARY WET FLY

The basic form of wet-fly fishing has been called, with some justice, the "chuck-and-chance-it" method. The fisherman simply mounts one, two or three wet flies on his leader, casts them across and slightly downstream and allows them to be swung round by the drag of current on the line, usually jerking his rod top a little in the hope of imparting a lively action to his fly or flies. When the cast is fished out—that is, when the line has straightened out below him—he takes two steps downstream and repeats the process. In this way he is effectively "covering the water," sweeping it from side to side so that the fish, wherever they may be, must inevitably see his flies.

This is a perfectly good way of fishing, so far as it goes, but it is only the beginning. Any fisherman who thinks at all will begin to depart from it and vary it almost at once. He will form ideas of where the fish are most likely to be lying and will give these places special attention. He may notice rising or feeding fish and cast to them. He will probably try to work his fly faster or slower or to give it a different action by different movements of his rod top. He will almost certainly notice that fish often take his fly just as it straightens out below him or just as he starts to retrieve it for the next cast. As soon as he is doing all these things he is really fishing and really enjoying himself.

NYMPH FISHING

In orthodox wet-fly fishing the fly is worked or allowed to work across the current. In nymph fishing it is, so far as possible, allowed to drift with the current. The simplest way to achieve this is to cast the fly more or less upstream and let it drift back, recovering line through the rings of the rod in the left hand. Since there is no pull of the current to break the surface film and draw the fly under, it is important that a nymph be lightly dressed, so as to sink immediately. Some nymphs are tied with a turn or two of lead or copper wire under the dressing to sink them more promptly.

The idea of the nymph is usually to represent the fly in the stage when it is rising to the surface to dry off and break out its wings—a time when it is particularly available to the fish. Ideally, then, the artificial nymph should be moving at exactly the same speed as the current and rising slowly through it. Unfortunately, the fisherman has to settle for the first part of this movement, the drift, because the second part can rarely be achieved artificially, though it is highly stimulating to the fish. It is achieved as the fly straightens out at the end of an ordinary wet-fly cast and one can make something of it by recovering a floating line at a speed very slightly greater than that of the current after the nymph has been allowed to sink well down in an upstream cast. But on the whole it is best to avoid any attempt at artificial movement and simply drift the nymph.

Since a fly drifted back from an upstream cast comes downstream pretty much in a straight line, it does not search the water as thoroughly as does the swing of an ordinary wet fly. For this reason a nymph fisherman must know his river and its likely places better than the ordinary wet-fly fisherman unless the fish are showing as they take the nymphs— bulging the surface with underwater "rises" or breaking it with their tails. Under these circumstances, which occur more often with brown trout than with other fish, upstream nymphing is a most delicate and satisfying art.

Yet another difference between nymph fishing and orthodox wet-fly fishing is in the fisherman's detection of and response to the strike of the fish. In ordinary wet-fly fishing the line is kept more or less tight between fly and rod top by the pull of the current, so the strike is felt. The response is to raise the rod top and tighten the line still more, thus setting the hook in the jaw of the fish. In upstream nymph fishing the line is slack and must be kept so to avoid interfering with the natural drift. The fisherman must detect the strike of the fish in one of three ways: by seing the bulge or tail rise of the fish at the moment he thinks his nymph is in place, by catching some glint of the fish's underwater movement if it is too deep for this, or by watching the float of his line and reacting to its least check against the current. The response, again, is to raise the rod point and set the hook, but this will be effective only if the line has been recovered in the left hand through the drift of the cast at a speed accurately calculated to the speed of the current. At best the lift of the rod top must be rather more positive than is the case with the ordinary wet fly, but since one is setting the hook into the fish, which is facing upstream, rather than away from it, the chance of effective hooking is considerably improved in spite of the other handicaps.

GREASED-LINE FISHING

The technique of greased-line fishing was developed in Scotland, for Atlantic salmon in low water. The purpose is to fish a small, lightly dressed fly just under the surface film, across the current but with an absolute minimum of drag from the pull of the line.

To achieve this the line and about two-thirds of the leader should float and the fly must sink as soon as it touches the water. The cast is made across or slightly upstream with a slack line. As the current draws the slack, a belly of line begins to form downstream. The fisherman must lift this before it begins to pull on the fly and roll it over upstream, without disturbing the fly in its drift. This movement, which is called "mending the line," is not so hard as it sounds. The lift is made by a wrist movement which brings out the spring of the upper part of the rod and is continued over in a smooth semi-circle at shoulder height, *placing* the line upstream rather than actually rolling it.

When all this is done properly, the fish usually rises through the water, intercepting the drift of the fly rather than striking at it. The proper response is not to lift the rod, but to leave it pointing downstream so that a belly forms in the line and the drag of the current on this draws the point of the light hook back into the corner of the fish's mouth. I have found this technique extremely effective for summer steelhead and large migratory cutthroat trout in the low water of summer and fall, as well as for Atlantic salmon. It would probably be effective for other fish, such as the brown trout and eastern brook, under similar conditions.

CONTROLLING THE FLY

These three techniques make the complete wet-fly fisherman, but he is complete not so much in being able to handle each one individually as in being able to combine them all in his fishing and use each as it fills the purpose of controlling the underwater movement of his fly to his needs and wishes.

Orthodox wet-fly fishing, that is, the cast across and downstream that allows the fly to sweep round on the pull of the current, is rarely the most effective method. The motion it gives to the fly is for the most part artificial in character and is usually too fast for the fish. While fish of all predatory species, which include the trouts, salmons and basses, do chase and capture swiftly moving prey, they rarely prefer to do so. Most of their food is taken by interception of creatures that are drifting or at most moving rather slowly and erratically. The various means of controlling the fly in the water make it possible to produce these effects.

The most important single control is that of the left hand on the loop of line between the reel and the butt ring of the rod. The fly-fisherman's left hand is rarely at rest. Before the cast it recovers line in several loops to prepare for the lift. During the cast it maintains the line's tension at the rod top. As the cast is completed it releases line for the shoot. When the cast is fishing, it may pull line off the reel and release it through the rings of the rod to slow the fly and lengthen the drift; it may recover line to speed up the fly, by stripping to make the movement erratic or by some smooth, continuous movement, usually looping it over the outstretched thumb and forefinger, to keep it even; a length of line may be recovered to lead the fly upstream past a rock, released again to let it slide down into the edge of the eddy behind the rock. It is often wise to strip in two or three loops of line as the cast fishes out and the fly is directly downstream and immediately release them again. If a fish has followed the fly around he may take on the pickup or the dropback. And throughout the fishing of the cast, even if there is little manipulation of the line, the forefinger and thumb of the left hand give the surest and most sensitive touch for feeling any response from the fish. The alternative is to hold the line between the first and second fingers of the right hand and I admit I often do so; but it is usually a sign that the fish have been quiet and I am a little inattentive.

After the left hand, the rod hand and the length and flexibility of the rod itself are the most valuable means of control. While it is important to be able to cast a straight line, it is just as important to be able to cast a loose or slack line. This is achieved by checking the rod rather sharply at an angle of only twenty or thirty degrees beyond the vertical as an end to the forward cast. It may be exaggerated by drawing the rod back a little as the line and leader straighten out over the water and even more by sending a strong sideways vibration through the rod which sets the line down in a series of snaky curves.

As the cast is fishing the rod top is moved slowly round to follow the line. If the fly is working in comparatively slow water, with a run of faster water between it and the rod top, the wise fisherman "mends" his line upstream, to slow the drag of the current. If he is fishing into fast water across an eddy or very slow water, he may mend the line downstream.

Sometimes it is advisable to hold the rod quite high, to keep the line out of the conflicting current altogether. Sometimes the rod top will be lifted to keep the fly riding high in the water, sometimes it must be kept well down. Sometimes the desirable control may be achieved by moving the rod slowly upstream, parallel to the water, then dropping it back and perhaps paying out line at the same moment.

STREAMER FISHING

Streamer flies are tied on long-shanked hooks and generally represent small fish rather than insects. Many ordinary wet flies such as the silver doctor, teal and silver, mallard and silver are also good representations of small fish and in general I prefer them to streamer flies for most freshwater fishing.

Because they do represent small fish, all these flies should normally be fished with a fairly lively action; this is particularly true when the large fish are feeding selectively on good concentrations of small fish, such as migrating trout or salmon fry. But it is well to remember that there are many times when a minnow fly is best fished slowly and haltingly or even drifted with the current. All predatory fish are attracted by unusual movement that suggests injured or weak prey and a fly that is carefully slowed by mending line and other methods of control gives this effect. It is likely to be more effective than a lively fly in the warmer water of summer and fall or whenever the fish are not feeding on good concentrations of natural fry. In lakes a streamer fly will sometimes attract very large fish if it is allowed to sink deeply and then retrieved slowly to the surface.

Local advice as to the best method of fishing a streamer or silver-bodied fly, whether in fresh water or salt, is always worth seeking, since circumstances can vary widely. But the wet-fly fisherman soon learns to vary his methods of working any fly and he can usually discover for himself, by trial and error and close observation, which one is getting the best results under any given set of conditions.

THE DEEPLY SUNK FLY

In the cold of winter and early spring, when fish are not moving freely, it is important to get the fly well down in the water. A sinking line is a help in this, as are flies tied on heavy hooks or weighted with lead or copper wire. But there is a sharp limit to the effectiveness of these mechanical aids. Flies cannot be too heavily weighted or they become awkward and even dangerous to cast, especially in a wind; and the best of sinking lines will not do its work properly unless skillfully used.

In anything stronger than a very slow current, it is best to cast a slack line somewhat upstream of straight across and to mend the line upstream almost as soon as it is on the water. A sinking line cannot be mended fully and continuously, as can a floating line, but often one or two short mends are possible after the first one, and these can be helpful. The rest is a matter of using rod and arm and whatever variations of current there may be to delay the drag of the line against the stream as much as possible. I usually take two steps downstream while the cast is fishing round to help in this.

The cast should be allowed to fish completely round until the fly is directly downstream and the recovery should be slow and cautious, especially in very cold weather. If the light pluck of a following fish is felt, the fly should be dropped back at once. In a particularly favorable place it is sometimes well to recover three or four loops of line and release them again before the final recovery and lift, even if nothing has been felt. Loose line in the left hand is always helpful in fishing a deep fly, as it can be released at any time to slow the drag of the current and its release usually permits another short upstream mend.

I am not suggesting that full familiarity with all these diverse techniques is essential to successful wet-fly fishing. There are times and places where the old, orthodox method of simply swinging the fly or flies across the stream will take plenty of fish. On some waters the upstream nymph may be the only variation needed from dry-fly fishing. But the wet-fly fisherman who would like to be effective under all conditions will be wise to master every possible means of controlling his fly. Such power of control not only increases his effectiveness, but adds immeasurably to his pleasure.

Wet-fly fishing at its best is a most rhythmic and satisfying performance. The competent fisherman can work over a length of stream with a minimum of interruption, changing his type of cast automatically to meet the conditions, working his fly into every likely place and giving the fish every possible chance to respond to it. These skills, besides being happy things in themselves, free him for his greatest pleasure, which is observation.

The power of observation, besides being a great source of pleasure, is the keenest tool in fishing of all kinds. Any good fisherman is observing constantly throughout his fishing, recording his observations in the recesses of his mind and comparing them with the observations of other days. The wet-fly fisherman watches his water carefully, noticing every stir and crease in its surface, every eddy and set of current. He watches for insect life and for signs of fish moving. He follows the swim of his fly as closely as he can. All this develops his knowledge and understanding of stream or lake conditions and builds the store of experience that directs the use of his technical skills.

The ultimate test of his skill as an observer comes when a fish responds to his fly. He must note and remember, if he can, how and where the fish came at the fly, how his cast was made and how his fly was fishing—what he himself was doing with his hands and his line and his rod. In the excitement of hooking and playing the fish, it is easy to forget these things. But they are the surest guide to a sound choice among his various techniques, not only for that particular day but for other days in the future when he comes upon similar conditions.

CHAPTER TEN

Dry-Fly Fishing

THE DRY FLY may be defined as any fly which floats on or in the surface film. May flies, stone flies, sedges and other aquatic insects float securely, their feet standing on the film; land creatures such as bees, ants and termites struggle against the unfamiliar element until their legs break through the film, which then supports their bodies for a while longer until at last they sink and drown. The dry fly, the artificial floating fly, may represent either type of creature in all stages except the last.

Dry-fly fishing was developed to its first perfection on the chalk streams of southern England. These clear and gentle streams, fed from the natural reservoirs of the chalk hills, flow for the most part through meadowland over gravel beds broken by patches of trailing weed that are full of insect life. The fish are brown trout that hold to firm positions in the current and wait for the nymphs and floating flies to be carried down to them. Often they are clearly visible to the angler; if not, they reveal themselves during hatches of fly by gentle, dimpling rises repeated over and over again at the same spot.

All this is ideal for the classic practice of the dry fly—the matching of the artificial fly to the hatch, the careful stalk of a feeding fish, the exact presentation of a small fly on a fine leader from a downstream position. In a sense it is easy fishing because the fisherman's greatest problem, finding his fish, is readily solved. But chalk-stream brown trout are shy fish and are often highly selective. An inept stalker or a clumsy caster will put one fish after another off the feed and catch nothing. Sometimes a fish will refuse every pattern shown him, no matter how perfectly presented, while rising steadily to natural insects. Once hooked, a big brown trout is likely to make for the nearest weed bed or other familiar shelter and with a light leader it is easy enough to lose him. So chalk-stream fishing is by no means simple; in fact, it may well be the most exacting of all training grounds for the fly-fisherman.

Dry-fly techniques crossed the Atlantic in the last decade of the nineteenth century and it soon became apparent that they had to be considerably adapted to meet North American conditions. The insect life, the swift and turbulent streams and the fish themselves were all different. In the East, Theodore Gordon was the greatest of the adapters and others like George M. La Branche and E. R. Hewittt made important contributions. In the West we are still learning and adapting, but there can be no doubt that wherever trout and grayling swim, the dry fly has its place. It is effective for Atlantic salmon on the East Coast and for steelhead on the Pacific Coast. It will take grayling and whitefish in arctic waters and goldeyes in the prairie provinces. Its satisfactions and excitements are so great that most fishermen prefer it whenever the fish are reasonably inclined to co-operate.

PREPARING EQUIPMENT

To fish a dry fly with any comfort and success, a floating line is essential. This means either one of the specially made floating lines, whose specific gravity is less than that of water, or a well-greased silk (intermediate) line. I have found it advisable, though not essential, to grease the floating lines as well as the silk lines.

A solid-line grease, such as the well-known Mucilin, preferably with a silicone base, is desirable in either case. Silk lines should be greased only when thoroughly dry and the grease is best applied with the thumb and forefingers. Draw the front fifty or sixty feet of line through the fingers several times, maintaining a light even pressure, until the whole length is smoothly coated. Leave this for a few minutes so that the grease can soak in, then draw the line through a soft cloth several times to clean off excessive grease. So greased and properly handled in casting, a silk line should float through a good long fishing day. A floating line may be greased much more lightly, but it also should be wiped clean of excessive grease.

In wet-fly fishing, especially during summer and fall, a floating line is often desirable and the same method of greasing applies. Both wet- and dry-fly fishermen who use greased lines are sometimes troubled by floating leaders. While I have taken many fish when the leader was floating and even prefer a floating leader with a dry fly in very fast and broken water, I agree that a floating leader is generally undesirable. Drawing the leader through soft mud will clear off any grease that has been transferred from the line and so permit the leader to sink. An alternative is to carry a small sample tube of tooth paste and clean the leader with this.

Most dry-fly fishermen oil their flies to help in keeping them afloat. Here, too, I have found that a silicone-base dressing is best; the ideal method is to dip a number of likely flies the night before and allow them to dry thoroughly. In addition, it is usually just as well to carry in one's fishing vest one of the small bottles that come with a brush in the stopper, to anoint flies by the waterside.

THE ORTHODOX DRY FLY

The first difficulty in all dry-fly fishing, in spite of the help of oil and grease, is to keep the line and fly floating well. This is achieved by making a number of false casts, that is, casts that keep fly and line in the air, before every cast that drops the fly on the water. False casting is the dry-fly fisherman's hallmark. He never lets his fly touch the water except in a working cast, while the good wet-fly man keeps his fly in the water as much as possible, to make sure it sinks instantly when he makes a working cast.

While there is no essential difference between casting a dry fly and a wet fly, it is usually rather more important that a dry fly land gently on the surface of the water, to avoid frightening the fish and to keep it from breaking the surface film and sinking. To achieve this the cast is made to a point a foot or two above the water, directly over where the fly is expected to land. Shooting a few coils of line makes this easier and produces a still softer effect. It is possible to go a step further and make the fly curl over so that it touches the water ahead of the line and leader, but this is not an essential refinement. The essentials are the smooth forward cast, the shoot that lays out line, leader and fly in a straight line parallel to the surface of the water, and the slight drop of hands and rod that permits it to light.

Accuracy is no more important in dry-fly fishing than in wet-fly fishing, though it seems to be because the dry-fly fisherman is so often casting to a rising or visible fish or to a spot where he thinks one will rise.

Accuracy of direction is not difficult to achieve, except in very bad winds. Accuracy in distance is considerably more difficult to judge and therefore to achieve, especially in fairly long casts. The one really serious error is overcasting the fish, bringing the line instead of the fly down within his circle of vision. To avoid this most fishermen, when in doubt, make a test cast that drops the fly on the water well short of the fish. From this it is comparatively easy to judge the proper distance. Most authorities consider that a fly dropped within a twenty-inch circle of a rising fish is close enough to attract his attention. Much greater accuracy than this is, of course, possible and sometimes necessary. But it is also true that a fish rising from any considerable depth may see and respond to a fly that is a good deal farther away.

When this cast has been made, upstream or upstream and across, to the rising fish or the chosen spot, it is allowed to drift back with the current. The rod should be held roughly parallel to the surface of the water. The left hand must take in line through the rings of the rod to keep pace with the downstream drift of the fly. If all this is done, the fisherman will be in position to raise his rod point, tighten the line and set the hook in any fish that rises faithfully to his fly. With small fish a rather rapid strike is necessary; with larger fish, which rise more deliberately, the strike that sets the hook should be proportionately deliberate. But neither is likely to be effective unless the left hand has picked up the slack line as it forms with the downstream drift of the fly, thus permitting the lift of the rod to tighten on the fish.

DRAG AND ITS CONTROL

The chief plague of the orthodox dry-fly fisherman is "drag"—that is, any pull of the current on the line which moves the fly across the stream, holds up its drift or pulls it downstream faster than the current. A sophisticated fish will rarely take a dragging fly and he may be put off the feed altogether by it. For this reason it is important not to recover line too fast with the left hand and most orthodox dry-fly men allow the fly only a short drift before picking it up, to dry it off by false casting and then cast again.

But even on a short drift, drag is very likely to occur unless one takes steps to control it or delay it. One of the commonest and most favorable dry-fly situations is the cast to a fish rising at the edge of a run under the far bank. Almost invariably the water in the body of the run is slightly faster than at the edge, where the fish is rising. If the fisherman casts his fly straight across, or even across and upstream on a straight line, there is bound to be almost instantaneous drag —often imperceptible to the fisherman, but nearly always disconcerting to the fish.

"Invisible" drag of this sort occurs in many other less obvious situations, so the experienced dry-fly fisherman rarely casts a straight, tight line to a fish or a favorable lie. He prefers to have a little slack, so that there will be time for the fly to float freely over the fish before the current takes effect.

The sidearm or backhand cast (depending on which bank one is fishing from) is a great help in this, since it tends to throw an upstream curve in the line. If an overhead cast is used a slight check in the forward cast, just before the fly lands, will also give enough slack to counteract moderate drag. Any cast deliberately aimed to throw a curve that will bring the fly over the fish ahead of the leader is also extremely effective in delaying drag.

These are measures that the experienced dry-fly fisherman uses all the time, without giving them conscious thought. Extreme situations, such as a cast across a fast run to a fish in slack water or a back eddy, simply call for more slack line. This can be achieved by an earlier check of the rod on the forward cast and also by giving it a side-to-side motion as the line shoots. Sometimes it is possible to mend the line and delay the drag still further, but in extreme situations the delay can never be long and the cast must be accurately made if the fish is to take the fly in time.

Controlling drag is one of the real pleasures and satisfactions of dry-fly fishing, but one should not be in a hurry to accept a situation where difficult control is called for. Often one's position can be considerably improved by moving to change the angle of the cast and sometimes it may be wise to pass up a fish altogether until there is a chance to try him from the opposite bank.

CHAPTER ELEVEN

Dry-Fly Fishing—New Techniques

I HAVE SUGGESTED that the orthodox dry-fly fisherman casts "to a likely spot," as well as to rising fish. Actually this is the first stage away from the strictly orthodox. It is used even on chalk streams, where a fisherman knows the feeding places of certain fish and sometimes puts a cast over them in the hope that "he may be there," even though no rise has been seen. The three native trout of North America, the eastern brook, the rainbow and the cutthroat, rarely rise as regularly, steadily and selectively as does the brown trout of Britain and Europe. For this reason, and also because rising fish are more difficult to spot in turbulent water, the North American fisherman soon took to searching the water with a dry fly.

SEARCHING THE WATER

This search begins in orthodox form, with the fisherman working upstream, casting upstream, choosing his spots with care, allowing his fly a comparatively short drift, avoiding drag and the risk of showing his line to a fish. This is undoubtedly the best way to go about it, especially on streams where the fish are shy and sophisticated. The fisherman is giving himself the best possible chance of rising any fish he covers and of hooking any fish he rises. He is also disturbing the fish as little as possible by his passing and so leaves a better chance for others who come along after him—or himself should he return later in the day.

The first refinement of this method of careful search is George La Branche's idea of "creating an artificial hatch." For this the fisherman must have complete confidence that a certain favored spot is holding a fish. He may even have seen the fish and have decided that he is not, for the moment, feeding. The purpose then becomes to cast the fly again and again to an exact spot, upstream of the fish and usually a little to one side of him, so that the drift over him and past him is always along exactly the same line.

This method calls for perfect casting, extreme accuracy and a certain amount of patience. It is often affective. Sometimes only a few casts are necessary to bring the fish up to the fly. Sometimes La Branche used "upwards of fifty." I don't think I have ever been quite so persistent, but I have risen fish after twenty or thirty casts to the same place and I have also been able to rise fish again within fifteen or twenty minutes of hooking and losing them, which seems a significant test. If the fish can be seen, he frequently offers encouraging signs: perhaps a quivering of the pectoral fins, perhaps a slight increase in the movement of his tail, perhaps a quick circle and return to his position. Any lifting in the water, combined with these other signs, almost certainly means that he will take within another cast or two.

SPIDER FISHING

The long, fine hackles and small hook of the spider fly give the fisherman two important advantages: the fly settles so lightly that it can be set down without disturbance on the stillest, smoothest water; once down, its pressure on the surface film is so slight that it can be given artificial movement without seeming unnatural to the fish.

I have found spider fishing exciting and satisfying, as well as highly effective with all trout, including summer steelhead. The flies float extremely well and are taken readily without artificial movement—in fact, a normal drift is preferable under most conditions and I always give it a chance before trying movement. The movement, imparted by a steady lift of the rod top or a gentle pull of the left hand on the line or both, may be slight enough to suggest the struggle of a natural fly to rise from the water or quite strong—

again, it is best to try only slight movement first. With a moderate wind it is possible to suggest a dapping movement, by holding the rod high and allowing the wind to pick the fly up, drop it to the water and pick it up again. But the spider is, perhaps, at its best on the tail slicks of good holding pools and over deep, glass-smooth, slow-moving canyon water. I have occasionally moved fish from the bottom up through ten feet or more of clear water in the middle of a hot summer day by persistently offering a spider. I doubt if it would have been possible with any other type of fly. I have also found spider fishing very successful on lakes, where movement of a surface fly may draw a fish's attention from some distance away.

THE HAIR-WING FLY, OR ANYTHING GOES

It will be seen that we have come a longish way from an imitation of the natural fly, cast upstream to a rising fish and floated over him without the slightest drag or artificial movement. I am not sure whether the hair-wing dry fly was developed first on the Atlantic salmon streams of the East or the rough and rocky trout streams of the West, but I suspect it was the latter, if only because the need was greater; and I remember an abundance of hair-wing flies in the West when the Pink Lady was still the Atlantic salmon fisherman's favorite.

Hair-wing flies float rough water better than any others, better than the best of spiders or variants tied with the finest Andalusian hackles. Fish like them in large sizes—I regularly use No. 6 hooks for summer steelhead and Nos. 8 and

10 are usually about right for rainbow and cutthroat trout, as well as brown trout in fast water.

These large hair flies not only float better, but are more easily seen in broken water. They do not drag under water nearly so easily as flies made of feathers and if they do drag under they can often be made to surface again when the pull of the line is slacked off.

All these qualities make them ideal for long drifts, for fishing downstream when an upstream approach is impossible and for the deliberate use of drag to stir fish up to the surface. Under western conditions I have found that the fish seldom refuse them, even when they are feeding on natural flies a good deal smaller. They will also bring very large fish up to the surface in lakes, especially when a good wind is blowing.

In fast-water dry-fly fishing it is well to observe all the usual dry-fly rules—work upstream if possible, look for rising fish or visible fish, keep the fly from dragging, search likely places without disturbing less likely ones. Under most conditions, these rules produce the best results. But if following the rules does not produce results or if conditions make it impossible to follow them, one should be prepared to try something else.

In fast water I have noticed that fish very often allow the fly to drift past them, then turn back to take it. Summer steelhead and migratory cutthroat, for instance, sometimes come back as much as twenty feet. For this reason I give the fly the longest possible drift, often allowing it to go past me downstream, mending the line to delay drag and even paying out some of the line I have recovered in my left hand. At the end of the drift the fly will, of course, drag round on the pull of the line until it is straight downstream. If the rod point is kept fairly well up, it will ride on top of the water and can be picked up by a simple forward cast. One then makes a few false casts to shake any excess of water from line and fly, takes a step or two to a new position, and is ready to make the next cast.

In fishing downstream, the cast is usually somewhat across and one checks the rod on the forward cast to make slack line for the drift. Sometimes it is possible to pay out a little more line from the left hand. Usually it is possible to mend the line once or twice, even if doing so gives the fly a little hop on the water. In this way a fairly long drift is possible, but in the end drag is inevitable. The best thing usually is to accept it and make use of it.

When possible I try to do this by giving the fly a fairly quick pull with the rod that allows me to slack off at once and let it drift freely back for a few feet, so that any fish attracted by the motion will have a chance to take on the natural float. When the fly has swung directly below me, I recover in the same way, a few feet at a time, letting the fly back a little at each recovery. Sometimes it is possible to give the fly a bouncing movement upstream against the wavelets of a strong current and then let it drift back. This can be very effective. With a strong downstream wind the fly can be raised from the water by lifting the rod top as high as possible, and then dropping it back. This also is likely to appeal to the most reluctant fish.

Though I consider this sort of thing useful tactics in rough water that one has already fished over in more orthodox ways, I do not think it is fair or likely to be very effective in quieter streams. There it simply disturbs the fish and makes everything more difficult for fishermen who follow after. While a dragging dry fly, properly handled, can be surprisingly attractive to fish, the fish that come to it often miss the fly completely or are missed on the strike by the fisherman—which means much the same thing: they have not taken with confidence. Fished upstream with a natural drift, the dry fly will rise more fish and hook more fish under nearly all conditions. But it is important to know that there are ways of fishing it downstream with good success and that the dry-fly man's enemy, drag, is something to be put to use when it cannot be avoided—and, occasionally, even when it can be avoided.

THE COMPLETE FLY-FISHERMAN

While I am perfectly prepared to respect the dry-fly purist or the wet-fly specialist, I do not feel that either is a complete fly-fisherman. There are times and places where the dry fly is the ideal method and yields the strongest possible satisfaction—it is nearly always a greater delight, for instance, to see a fish come to one's fly than merely to feel him. But there are other times and other places where the wet fly is not only far more effective but offers special pleasures and challenges that the dry-fly purist will never know— the cunning search of freshet-swollen water for instance, or the precise and breathless handling of a greased-line fly over a known steelhead or salmon lie in dead low water.

Similarly, it seems to me wise to understand as many individual techniques within each art as one is likely to have use for. All of them have their uses—I have taken English chalk-stream trout on downstream drifts and even by deliberate use of drag, migratory cutthroats with orthodox dry flies, Pacific salmon by greased line and steelhead with spiders—and all have their own special delights, their own particular revelations of fish responses and behavior.

They should not become a burden, any more than the understanding and use of several different ways of casting should be a burden. It is best, I think, to start with the more orthodox techniques, perfect these and learn others one at a time, as the need for each is felt. In this way they become a reservoir of skill, ready to be drawn on at any time and put to use almost instinctively when conditions call for them. Casting a fly well has its keen satisfactions and is always important, but it is only the beginning. The choice of where to put the fly, how best to bring it over the fish, how to control it to one's own ends among the complexities and changes of current, how to respond when the fish rises or strikes—these things are the essence of fly-fishing, and the more a fisherman knows of them the greater his pleasure is likely to become.

CHAPTER TWELVE

Hooking and Playing Fish

WHEN THE FISH HAS TAKEN his fly or lure
or bait, the fisherman usually responds by "striking" to set the hook. Essentially this action is a
raising of the rod top to tighten the line and so pull the point
of the hook, beyond its barb, into the fish's jaw.

In downstream wet-fly fishing this is usually a simple
matter. The least move of the rod top will produce an equal
movement of the fly—either directly, when the fly is more

or less straight downstream, or around the curve of the line
if the fly is still swinging across on the current. I think of this
as simply tightening on the fish, rather than striking him.
The important thing is not to hurry the response, unless the
fish are quite small; larger fish usually take quite deliberately and give one plenty of time to set the hook. Very often
the pull of the current on the line is, by itself, enough to set
the hook firmly when it is on the swing, and even when the
fly is straight downstream a fish will often strike himself by
turning back as, or just after, he takes it. The important
thing at such times, if the fish is at all large, is to be ready
to release instantly any line held in the left hand and let the
pull of the fish come on to the ratchet of the reel as soon as
possible.

With the dry fly, the nymph or the upstream wet fly,
striking is rather more difficult, since the line is constantly
drifting back towards the fisherman and creating slack between the rod top and the fly. This slack must be steadily recovered by the fisherman's left hand during the drift of the
fly, yet the recovery must not be too fast or it will drag the
fly. When the fish rises the right hand must respond, not to
what it feels, but to what the eye sees. The response, again,
is a lifting of the rod top to tighten on the fish, but it must
be properly calculated to take up the slack line. In slow,
quiet streams, this is usually not much and the fisherman
must be sure not to tighten so hard that he breaks the light
leader he is probably using. In fast water there is often altogether too much slack, and the fisherman may find himself not only lifting his rod point as high as it will go, but
frantically hauling line with his left hand. No moment in

fly-fishing is more exciting and satisfying than that of a strike perfectly timed to the deliberate rise of a really big fish.

PLAYING FISH

Once the fish is hooked, what one does with him depends on his size, the strength of the leader and the current, obstructions and other features of the water. The fly-fisherman is rarely fishing with tackle strong enough simply to haul a fish in. He must depend on the spring of his rod, he must yield line promptly to any strong rush and he must take full control only when the fish has tired itself sufficiently to be no longer dangerous.

I try to fish always with the strongest leader I think the fish will stand for, but it is wise always to give them the benefit of the doubt on this point; it is better to hook a fish and lose him than not rise him at all because the leader is too heavy. On western streams, where one may go fishing for two- or three-pound cutthroat trout and often rise a ten-pound coho salmon or steelhead instead, I have learned that large and vigorous fish can be landed with ease and comparative certainty on leaders as fine as 1x or 2x, even in fast water. On quiet meadow streams the difficulties of handling big fish on light gear are really no less than in fast water, because such streams are usually full of weeds and other obstructions which the fish quickly turn to for shelter when they feel the hook. At the same time the relatively smooth surface of the water, its clearness and the feeding habits of the fish are likely to call for the finest possible leader, so the fisherman may well be at a greater disadvantage in what seems to be the easier water.

Once the fish is hooked and has made his first run, it is time for the fisherman to take charge. This consists of exerting all the pressure the gear will stand and trying to lead him to where one wants to net him or beach him. If the fish is of any size it is still necessary to be ready to let him take line again at the least sign of vigorous resistance. In this way, by alternately yielding and recovering line, the fish is gradually exhausted. As his struggles become easier to control it is time to begin thinking of how to land him.

NETTING OR BEACHING A FISH

The first sign that a fish is nearly ready for net or beach is when his rushes are easily stopped and when an even pressure of the rod will lift his head. He is not fully ready for either operation until the rod will lift his head right to the surface and draw him along on his side. It is perfectly possible to hurry this operation with small fish, but extremely unwise to do so with larger fish. Similarly, a smallish fish— a trout of a pound or less, for instance—can be drawn upstream towards the net against a moderate current, but it is as well not to attempt this with a leader finer than 2x or with a fish much larger than a pound.

If possible, the fisherman should find an eddy or fairly sheltered water in which to net his fish. When it is quiet on its side or unable to do more than thrash a little on the surface the fisherman should slide his net into the water and hold it still in his left hand while the rod in the right hand draws the fish over the net. As soon as it is well over he need only lift the net to finish the affair. It is always wrong to stab at the fish with the net or to chase him with it, as any movement of this sort will almost certainly stir him to further activity and the risk of breaking the leader on a short line, especially in the excitement of overeagerness, is very great.

To beach a fish one should choose a gradual slope of sand or gravel if possible, though almost any slope will do. The principle is much the same as in netting. The fish must be exhausted and under full control. He should be led in on his side, with his head up, directly towards the beach, so that his head is stranded on the slope. As soon as he feels the gravel under him he will make an effort to swim and this will push him up the slope, out of the water. So long as a gentle, even strain is kept on his head every movement he makes will take him farther out of the water until at last he is high and dry on his side. All one has to do then is walk down and pick him up.

Beaching fish calls for a little more judgment and delicacy of touch than netting them, but it is really quite a simple operation on any stream that has good gravel bars or shelving banks. A net is a necessity only when one is wading and does not want to come out of the water every time a fish is hooked, when a stream has steep-cut banks or when fishing from a boat. Sometimes a fly-fisherman finds himself hooked into a fish that is much too large for his net, with no very suitable place at hand for beaching. Some fish, such as the Atlantic salmon and the Pacific spring salmon, can be quite readily and securely "tailed"—that is to say, gripped and lifted by the "wrist" or narrowest part of the body immediately above the tail. Again the fish must be played to exhaustion and it is best to use the right hand for a firmer grip. Large trout such as steelhead can also be tailed, but it takes a much stronger grip to do it, because the wrist above the tail is much thicker and the outer rays of the tail itself close in and do not give the same purchase. It is altogether safer to "gill" such fish— that is, to slip a finger under the gill plate of the fish and lift it out head first.

JUMPING FISH

Two rather old-fashioned precepts for playing a hooked fish should be examined at this point. The first is, "Keep the rod point well up," and the second, "Always keep a tight line." Neither is sound as it stands.

The rod point should be kept up, but only far enough to maintain an even bend throughout its length. Under most conditions this means that a line drawn from the rod hand to the tip of the rod, disregarding its bend, would be at an angle of something less than forty-five degrees from the horizontal. This brings the maximum power to bear on the fish with the least possible risk of breaking anything. Excessive raising of the rod point puts the chief strain on the top one-third of the rod's length.

The injunction to "keep a tight line" on the fish has a certain general application in that one should try to maintain at least some pressure in order to tire the fish as quickly as possible. But giving slack line does not, as some anglers believe, "allow the fish to spit out the hook." If the hook has been properly set, beyond the barb, in a solid part of the fish's mouth, there is not the least likelihood of his spitting it out or shaking it loose or getting rid of it in any way at all; in fact, the angler himself often finds it difficult to free when the fish is landed. It is well to remember this, because there are many occasions when it is good tactics to slack off on a hooked fish.

Jumping fish are often disturbing to the nerves of the inexperienced fisherman, or even to the experienced. The old rule here is: "drop the rod point"—in other words, slacken the line—and it is sound. A jumping fish does quite often shake the hook. In my opinion he does so not because he is jumping, but because he has been hooked in the tongue or some other soft and sensitive place, which is precisely why he is jumping in the first place. This is particularly likely to be true of a fish that goes off in a wild series of jumps as soon as the hook is set. He may free himself anyway by tearing the hook free against the resistance of the line in the water. He will certainly do so if any attempt is made to keep a tight line on him. The only real hope the fisherman has is to offer a minimum of resistance and let him tire himself, then handle him as gently as possible towards the net or beach.

The jumping of a well-hooked fish offers little danger, provided the line is left to run freely to him. Dropping the rod point can help in this. If the jump is allowed to come suddenly against a tight line the probability is not that the hook will be torn out but that the leader will break.

SULKING AND OBSTRUCTIONS

The main purpose of keeping pressure on a hooked fish is to keep him moving and so tire him out. Most fish react to the strain of the line by trying to swim against it. If the strain is too light a fish may work himself down to the bottom and stay there—a frustrating business known as "sulking." A strain from a different angle may move a sulking fish, but it is better to give him no chance to go down and set himself.

One may use strain also to turn a fish away from a weed bed, a log jam or some other obstruction. Sometimes the fish is too strong and reaches his shelter in spite of all the strain the fisherman dares to use. The best course then is to slack off altogether and let him swim his own way out. Surprisingly often he will do so. The fisherman should watch closely and pull him off balance and away from the obstruction the moment he is free of it.

Often a fish will run down to the tail of the pool and there, with the help of the current, keep going strongly and force the fisherman to follow him. There is no harm in this provided it is possible to follow. Sometimes it is not possible or there is risk of the line tangling in the rocks or other obstructions of the shallow water beyond the tail of the pool. Here again a slack line may work wonders, if tried soon enough—that is, before the fish is caught in the really strong draw of the current. Slack should be given generously—line should be stripped off the reel and allowed to drift down so that it forms a belly below the fish. The drag of the current then exerts a strain from dowstream and there is an excellent chance the fish may swim up against it.

When a fish is holding in dangerously fast water at the tail of a pool it may be too late to give slack. In this case the most effective move is to maintain a steady strain and walk very slowly upstream. The fish will usually follow. How effective this can be I once learned from walking a thirty-pound salmon more than two hundred feet upstream, in heavy water, with only the strain of a four-ounce fly rod.

Lastly, there is the fish that swims directly towards the fisherman. Usually the best thing here is to hand-line—that is, to strip in line as fast as possible with the left hand until the strain comes on the rod again. Both hand-lining and walking fish are useful means of easing them away from trouble of almost any kind. The main point is to maintain a steady tension so that the fish is led rather than forced away from his chosen position.

PUTTING FISH BACK

Few fly-fishermen today aim to fill a bag limit or to take many fish at all. They do not need to, because it is usually quite easy to return a fly-hooked fish unharmed to the water. It is best to avoid handling a fish that one wants to return, so I usually lead them to my right hand, take hold of the leader and slide the hand down to the hook shank. A vigorous twist will usually free it and allow the fish to swim away.

If this cannot be done I prefer to net or beach the fish and work the hook out with my right hand while holding his lower jaw between the thumb and forefinger of my left hand. Sometimes a fish that has been played hard and taken from the water is not ready to swim off. He should be nursed gently in the water with his head upstream until he recovers, holds himself steady and swims away. If the flow of current is not enough to restore the fish or if he is very much exhausted, it is sometimes necessary to draw him back and forth in the water to open the gill plates and start the gills working again.

Few things are more rewarding than to feel life returning in this way under the touch of one's hands. It gives a richer satisfaction than any number of dead fish and in no way dims the memory of the rise, the strike and the struggle that went before.

CHAPTER THIRTEEN

Fishing Streams

FOR MOST FLY-FISHERMEN a stream is the ideal place to fish. It offers variety, excitement, accessibility and a special intimate loveliness seldom available on a lake or salt water. A stream is just that to a casual observer —a pretty flow of water with life on its surface and growth on its banks. To a fisherman it is pools and runs and riffles, hidden rocks, sunken weed beds, gravel bars, log jams and cut banks. Its temperature and flow and color all have special meaning for him. He looks at the surface and reads the depths, judging where big fish should lie and where smaller ones, visualizing the float of his fly along a glide beyond an eddy, planning a cast that will reach far under the overhanging brush of the far bank or hang briefly near the sheltering rocks that break a run of fast water.

All this is streamcraft, and it is not learned from books; the stream itself and the fish that live in it are the ideal instructors. But there are some things that can be described in words to help shorten the practical learning.

THE ANATOMY OF A STREAM

Streams are highly complex. No stream has an even bottom or an evenly distributed flow from bank to bank. Some streams change from year to year as each season's floods and freshets gouge new pools, build new gravel bars, cut away banks and tear out new channels; others are relatively stable. But change is going on in even the quietest of them, for moving water is a powerful and persistent force.

The rocks and sandbanks and gravel bars of a stream slow and direct its flow. Each curve shifts the flow from one bank to the other. Each rapid speeds and aerates the water; each pool slows it again. It is among these signs and all their infinity of variation that the fly-fisherman looks to find his fish.

Fish are to be found holding either in resting places or feeding places. Feeding places are likely to be in runs of current, which gather the feed from wider and shallower stretches of quieter water above. But they may also be found in the easy water along the edge of a run or even in the back eddy formed by a run. Resting places may be at the bottom of deep pools or under cut banks or almost anywhere that the fish find sheltered water near bottom with a good flow of current over it.

THE ANATOMY OF A POOL

Pools, whether in rocky rivers or gravel rivers or meadow streams, are the likeliest holding places, because they offer the ease of moderate flow, the shelter and security of depth and a steady drift of feed from shallower, more productive waters above.

The simplest type of pool would be no more than a deepening of the stream in the middle of a straight stretch. Such a pool, in theory at least, would be absolutely symmetrical, with a run of water of some force coming in at its "head." Almost at once this run begins to spread out and slacken off into the "throat" of the pool. Halfway down the pool the spreading and slackening will be almost complete; the rush of current will have become a smooth, even flow over deep water and a back eddy, circling back towards the throat of the pool, will have formed on either side. I think of this part as the "spread of the pool." Finally, as the bottom begins to shelve upwards again, the current draws more swiftly and glides smoothly out over the "tail of the pool."

These four points, the head, the throat, the spread and the tail are the likeliest holding places for fish under normal conditions. Head, throat and tail are the likeliest feeding stations—feeding fish may be along the edge of the current on either side at the head and in the throat if the main flow is at all strong, and they may lie anywhere across the tail. Migratory, non-feeding fish such as Atlantic salmon and steelhead, are more likely to be found at the spread or in the tail. In high-water conditions both sides of the spread and along the edge of the eddies nearest the current are the likeliest places to look for feeding fish as well as resting fish. In very low water the head and throat of the pool may hold either resting or feeding fish in full daylight, though some fish are likely to drop down into the tail towards evening.

COMPLICATIONS WORTH CONSIDERATION

In practice, few pools are as simple and symmetrical as the one I have just described. Most pools are formed on curves, which means that the main flow of current, sweeping round against the outside of the curve, has worn itself a deep channel against the bank, while gravel has gradually built up in the back eddy on the inside of the curve. The run of water around the outside of the curve is an ideal feeding place because it collects nearly all the feed from the shallows above, while the overhanging trees and brush of the bank also contribute. At the same time it offers ready shelter in its depth and probably also under tangled roots and brush growing out from the bank. Runs of this type may also form on relatively straight stretches of stream where gravel bars or weed beds force the current into a narrow flow that cuts in against the bank. Wherever they occur, runs such as these instantly catch the eye of the experienced fly-fisherman.

Many pools are divided in some way, by large boulders or rock ledges or gravel bars. Such divisions may make several productive runs, all of which are worth careful examination. Some of the most productive pools I know have several minor runs of water entering at the head and angling over an apron of shallow water towards the main flow of current. Sometimes every one of these will hold one or more good fish waiting for the first fly that drifts over them.

There is, nearly always, a right and a wrong bank from which to fish any given pool or stretch of water. Some streams are so large that they can be fully covered only by fishing from both banks; others, even larger, only allow the fly-fisherman to reach a small section of their breadth. One simply treats these according to their merits, accepting the limitations, judging and exploring the water that can be reached as though it were a smaller stream within a large one. But on a stream that can be fully covered many places can be fished properly only from one bank.

Generally speaking, it is best to be on the inside of the curve, whether one is fishing the upstream dry fly or the downstream wet fly. In heavily brushed gravel streams this is almost essential, since the gravel bars on the inside of the curves make the only easy traveling, while the deep water, cut banks and heavy brush of the opposite side make it impossible to cover the fish without disturbing them. In summer and fall, when the water is low and the stream can be waded, this presents no special difficulty. But in high water it may mean that some pools are completely unfishable unless a crossing can be found by a bridge or a log jam. In meadow streams with clear banks the problem is much less serious— it is often an advantage to be able to work a run under one's own bank, especially in fishing a dry fly or a nymph upstream; the approach to the fish is good and the risk of drag may be much reduced.

Wading is an important part of stream fishing. In quiet streams it is best, if possible, to avoid wading at all since the risk of disturbing the fish may be considerable. Where wading is essential, it should be done cautiously, with due respect for the fish and one's own safety. It is important to avoid sending out unnatural ripples ahead of one's wading and equally important to avoid making underwater sounds by stumbling over rocks or using a metal-shod wading staff. Properly used, wading can give tremendous advantages, even apart from the extra reach it allows; one can place oneself to reduce the drag of a fast current, for instance, or to hang a wet fly over a particularly good place. But a clumsy wader may also do himself more harm than good by wading through water where his fly should be fishing or by approaching his fish too closely, especially from above.

It is well not to be too ambitious in wading until one has built up a good measure of experience and confidence. Currents can be deceptively strong; round boulders can be slippery and treacherous; loose gravel may slip away under the feet in a heavy current; the convenient bar that one wades so easily downstream may end with deep water on all sides and the return journey, against the stream, will not be so easy. It is well to remember things of this sort and grow into them gradually before taking any long chances. The most useful rule I know for all wading, under all conditions, is to place one foot absolutely securely before moving the other one. This is the best assurance of safety and it also means that all movements will be slow and deliberate, as they should be in approaching fish.

In crossing a stream of any force, start well up from the point you hope to reach on the far side. Crossing on an angle downstream is far easier and less exhausting than trying to hold against the current or make ground upstream. Working upstream with a fly, dry or wet, is far more difficult and tiring than working downstream, yet it is worth doing. Normally, in searching upstream or down, one takes about two good steps between each cast. Working downstream this is easy enough because the fly is in the water, any rise of a fish will be felt, so one's hands and eyes are free. Working upstream, especially with a dry fly, it is another matter altogether. One is moving against the current, which is of considerable significance in fast-flowing streams; the dry-fly fisherman cannot take his eyes off the fly while it is on the water ahead of him, and he does not want it to drag down and become sodden. Yet if he holds it in the air by false casting while he makes his upstream move, he risks making a misstep that will trip him or a miscast that will tangle his line or throw the fly against the rod. For these reasons I believe it is safest to let the fly swing round and trail behind on a short line, then choose one's footing and make the move before lifting the fly to dry it off and cast again. On a gentle stream with an even bottom one can move safely while false-casting, but even here the move should be made slowly and deliberately.

Some fishermen carry a wading staff when fishing fast water. It can be of great value in crossing a strong run or in finding footing among large boulders, and its use certainly reduces fatigue in a long day's fishing. It is, of course, a nuisance much of the time and one is inclined to let the matter go and pick up a stick when one is needed. But there are some rivers where the usefulness of a staff more than makes up for any inconvenience. The most satisfactory staff I have found is a one-inch aluminum alloy tube about four and a half feet long, fitted with a crutch tip and a bicycle handlebar grip. It should be carried on a shoulder strap that allows a full arm's reach so that it will drift downstream out of the way until it is needed.

THE FISH

It is very easy to overestimate the intelligence of a fish, but just as easy to underestimate his reaction time and the sharpness of his vision and other senses. All fish live in danger—from other fish, from birds and from mammals, including man himself. Any unusual movement, especially if it is abrupt, is likely to mean danger. A fisherman is well advised, then, to move deliberately and keep out of sight as much as he possibly can. Though a fish's vision of things above the water is limited to some extent by the mirror effect of the undersurface everywhere except directly above him, he can in fact see objects above the surface of the water at some distance away, and the higher they are above the water the farther he can see them. It is also of some importance that he sees better in front of him than behind.

The broken surface of a stream changes these effects somewhat, probably to the advantage of the angler, but they are still sound in general principle and it is well always to consider them. When possible, an upstream approach is desirable. And in any close approach, say within fifty feet, it is certainly advisable to keep well down, especially if fishing from a bank above the water level. Under these conditions, it is often well to crawl into place and make the cast from a kneeling or crouching position, keeping the rod low. A fisherman who thinks along these lines, respecting the sharpness of a fish's vision and the probability of his swift defensive reaction against any hint of danger, will always improve his chances of results.

TRIPPING THE REACTION

It is wise to think of fish as reacting rather than thinking. They react to danger by flight for shelter—into the depths of a pool or some other hiding place close at hand. Occasionally a feeding fish, especially a big brown trout, simply sinks down in the water at the angler's approach and gradually fades from sight. This is still a reaction, though its deliberate nature gives an impression of considered action, and it is the more effective in that it does not draw attention as does more violent flight.

If flight is the reaction to danger, pursuit is the reaction to food. The pursuit may be very active, as when the prey is a small fish or a fly that looks like one; or it may be calm and deliberate, as is the rise of a large trout to a drifting May fly. The point is that the mechanism of this reaction is built into the fish; he lives by it and has lived by it since he emerged from the egg and absorbed its yolk sac. Under certain conditions the reaction trips readily, in others it does not; but the fisherman should remind himself that it is always there, waiting for the proper stimulus. This may be a change of light, a hatch of insects or simply the sudden appearance of food or something that looks like food. George La Branche, casting his fly fifty times over a fish, was simply creating a set of conditions in which the reaction would trip.

Similarly, the wet-fly fisherman, working his fly at different speeds and depths, is looking for the combination that will trip the reaction; and every fly-fisherman who changes his fly hopes that the new pattern will do the same thing.

The dry-fly fisherman, because he so often can see his fish or knows exactly where it is lying, has the best chance of all to work on its moods. His most powerful means is in the exact placement of his fly. Normally a sidearm cast will serve him best in this because it keeps the rod low, brings the fly in sight of the fish at the last possible moment and permits him to throw an upstream loop in his line which delays drag and, when properly thrown, will bring the fly over the fish ahead of the leader. His normal cast should be aimed to set the fly on the water a foot or two upstream of a rising fish so that it will float down directly over him.

If this fails to produce a response he may try placing the fly slightly to one side or the other of his fish or he may cast well upstream to give it a longer float down to him; he may try dropping it as close as he can to the fish's nose or he may let it land somewhere near his tail. I have known all these variations to prove effective with fish that would not come to the orthodox first choice. The sidearm cast also has the effect of keeping the false casts that dry the fly out of sight of the fish, which is considered an advantage by most fishermen. But false casting can also be used to stimulate a fish. I have several times seen fish, in both streams and lakes, move over some distance to bring themselves under a fly that was repeatedly shown above the surface by a series of false casts. When the fly is finally allowed to light, such fish come to it at once.

Every fisherman, as his experience grows, develops a set of rules for himself and a number of firmly fixed ideas. Both the rules and the ideas, growing out of experience, are likely to be sound most of the time. But fish and their habits and preferences are predictable only up to a point. It pays to experiment, to break rules, to challenge theories, and one of the easiest ways of doing this is to master a number of different techniques in presenting and working the fly.

It is natural for any fisherman, fishing a familiar stream, to prefer the places where he has seen or hooked fish before. This is his experience, his stream knowledge, his most valuable possession. But it is unwise to be limited by it, because there are always new things to be learned about any stream. It pays to put a fly over the likely-looking spot that has never produced; it pays to work a pool through faithfully from end to end—a little difference in the height of the stream or its temperature, some shift of bottom in last season's floods, or even some whim of an individual fish, may produce a rise where there was never one before. It pays to explore side channels, to test a glide of smooth water in the middle of a rapid, to look for fish where someone else may not have looked for them.

In the last analysis, fish are where you find them, which

may or may not be where the book says they should be. A good fisherman respects the rules because they make sense most of the time. But he also knows how to vary them when they don't seem to be making sense to the fish. If the variations don't make any more sense than the rules themselves, no harm is done. But if one of them happens to pick up a fish, something has been added to experience.

CHAPTER FOURTEEN

Fishing Lakes

A FEW LAKES have shallow, firm-bottom shorelines or long, gravelly points and bars that favor wading, and these are delightful to fish. One can cover all the best of the water accurately and closely, moving easily to new ground, always knowing one's position and without too much concern for wind and weather. But such lakes are rare and most lake fishing is done from boats. Fly-fishing from a boat can be pleasant enough, but it calls for a few particular points of explanation.

CASTING FROM A BOAT

One is usually not alone in a boat. Lakes are windy places, and boats, even anchored boats, turn and twist and change direction with surprising ease. A fly securely hooked in the ear or the neck or the back of the hand is sufficiently unpleasant; in the eye it can be disastrous. Against this last, glasses or even a peaked hat or cap are good measures of protection. But the only real protection is sound and sensible casting.

I think it should be accepted that it is quite impossible for more than two fly-fishermen to fish at the same time from anything smaller than a fair-sized yacht. And in any boat less than twenty feet long, two fly-fishermen fishing together had better treat each other (and themselves) with a good deal of respect.

The first rule is to cast at right angles to the boat. The second is to separate as widely as possible. The third is to cast outside the boat—that is to say, if two right-handed fishermen are casting over the right gunwale, the sternman should be casting over his right shoulder, preferably with some modification of a sidearm cast, while the bowman should be casting backhanded over his left shoulder. All three of these rules can be varied with safety by good casters, but even good casters should only vary them after due consideration and with great respect.

Wind is probably the greatest hazard, a deeply sunk line the next and any sudden excitement, such as a big fish rising within reach, comes next. The answer is control, control of one's line and control of one's emotions. Wind, even of the most gusty and fitful kind, must be allowed for, which simply means reasonable precaution when conditions are bad. The drowned line, which can mean a badly mistimed pickup for the backcast and any degree of chaos from there on, should always be expected and allowed for. One feels the line as one prepares for the backcast; if there is the slightest doubt that it will come free under full control, the only sound thing to do is to bring it to the surface and free it by a short roll cast before attempting to lift it. Roll casting can be the full answer to many difficult conditions in boat fishing, especially those of strong and uncertain winds. The answer to emotional responses is much the same; one simply has to build in an automatic safety reaction that brings the line under full control before it is lifted into a position where it can do damage.

I don't want to overemphasize this matter of safety, but it is something that one owes to the boatman or partner who is handling the boat or to the fisherman who is sharing it. It is also the simplest way of drawing attention to the ordinary competence in casting and handling line that is so essential to the enjoyment of fly-fishing under any conditions. I will not concern myself here with the other aspects of safety afloat, such as a decent respect for weather, the provision of life preservers and a good set of oars, as well as some knowledge of how to use them, and such precautions as not overloading a boat or presuming too much upon its stability; these are matters of boating safety rather than fishing safety, and are better taught elsewhere. But they should be learned and well understood by anyone who ventures to fish from a boat on fresh or salt water. Fishing is meant to be a gentle sport, not unduly hazardous; but any mixture of ignorance and foolhardiness can make it both rough and fatal.

SEARCHING A LAKE

Depth, temperature and wind are the critical factors in lake fishing. The lake fisherman has a large area, or rather an enormous volume, of water to search; it is important for him to understand that not all of it is likely to be productive.

For the most part a fly-fisherman's concern is with water less than thirty feet deep—usually much less. He searches along the shelves of a lake's edges, over and along its weed beds, off its points, on its shoals and flats, off its stream and creek mouths. These are the productive places, for it is here in the shallows, for the most part, that the aquatic life on which fish depend for feed can thrive and multiply.

A very steep shoreline, plunging almost straight down into a lake, is generally a much less favorable place to search than a gradual slope that thrusts out a broad underwater shelf. Wherever a point of land thrusts out into a lake, there is almost certain to be a corresponding submerged point of rocks or gravel stretching out still further. The heads of bays usually have flats in front of them and creeks and streams are certain to have built up shoals off their mouths. All these places are particularly favorable and no fly-fisherman should disregard them. Equally favorable, though harder to find, are the shoals and flats that rise from the lake bed itself. Generally these are well known locally, but a fisherman on a strange lake can often guide himself by watching for a glimpse of the bottom through the water, by following out some likely line and testing it with his anchor or—best of all —by studying a contour map of the lake if one is available.

Temperature of both air and water is another useful guide. Most game fish prefer water temperatures of 60° F. or less and will seek them out if they are available. This means that the mouths of cold streams always bear watching in the summer months, as do any places where cold springs enter from underground. When surface temperatures are well over 60° F., trout will almost certainly be deep down in the cooler water, perhaps too deep for the fly except in the evenings. But a brisk wind lasting several hours can change this by stirring up some of the cooler water to mix with the surface water and by increasing the oxygen content of the surface water through wave action.

Excessively or unseasonably cold air and water conditions can also make for slow fishing, by slowing the hatching and movement of insect life and the metabolism of the fish themselves. But there are occasional surprises in this, especially in early spring, when fish become extremely active under bitterly cold conditions and take every fly thrown at them.

Wind is the lake fisherman's constant concern and almost constant companion. A steady, moderate wind that sets up a good surface ripple or even a constant, easy wave action, is ideal. Cold, gusty, changing winds are much less favorable and also very difficult to fish. Glassy calms are nearly always difficult and bad, though calm towards sunset can make for pleasant dry-fly fishing. If one must fish calm water in the middle of the day it is usually wise to get the fly well down.

Unless the wind is very rough, most lake fishermen prefer to fish along a lee shore—that is, one toward which the wind is blowing. The argument is that any floating feed will drift towards such a shore and that the water along it will be well oxygenated by the wave action. Such fishing calls for good boat handling and it is essential to have someone constantly at the oars or at the tiller of a slow-running outboard. In really heavy winds, fishing a lee shore is out of the question, but the chances are that the wind will be finding its way into normally sheltered places and the fishing will be just as good, as well as a great deal more comfortable, in partial shelter. In shallow, muddy lakes, where even moderate wave action stirs up the bottom silt, a lee shore is usually to be avoided.

FISHING A LAKE

The lake fisherman has three choices: he can anchor his boat, work it along under the power of oars or motor, or allow it to drift. He will probably use all three methods at different times and under different conditions.

Fly-fishing from an anchored boat is perfectly satisfactory in well-stocked waters and particularly favorable places. With a fairly long anchor line, especially if there is enough wind to swing the boat, a good deal of water can be covered from a single hold by paying out a little more line from time to time. When all the line is out, one simply hauls in the anchor and moves to a new position. It is wise to lift and drop the anchor with some care and wise at all times to avoid any bangings and clatterings of oars or other equipment against the sides or bottom of the boat, as sounds of this kind vibrate to considerable distances through the water.

Working a boat is best done with oars and is in itself an

interesting part of the sport for anyone who understands what he is doing. Working slowly along a shoreline or along the edge of a bar or weed bed is, in my opinion, the most satisfactory way of lake fishing. The boat should be moved slowly and steadily, within good casting distance of the shore or reef. If two fishermen are casting, one should be in the bow, the other in the stern, with the oarsman in the center seat of the boat. If there is only one fisherman, he should be in the stern, with the oarsman in the bow seat. Off a lee shore it is necessary to hold the bow at an angle to the wind to maintain an even distance from the shore itself.

The fisherman should be casting in towards shore, covering sunken logs and treetops, large boulders and other likely places with care. He should test different depths and methods of working the fly until he has found what seems to be the right one. It is usually a good thing to fish each cast well out—that is, to allow the movement of the boat, with the recovery of the line, to draw the fly off the shallows and over the drop-off until it straightens out behind the boat. A fish will often follow around and take just as the line straightens out.

If two men are fishing in this way the bowman can safely allow his line to fish round and straighten out along and behind the boat. The sternman should then lift his own line and cast over the bow line towards shore. As soon as the stern line is in the water, the bowman recovers his line from under the rod and line of the sternman and makes his new cast towards shore. This sets up a natural rhythm that can be maintained through a whole day's fishing without much risk of the lines tangling each other.

Drifting is also best done with someone at the oars, but given the right kind of breeze a boat can be placed to drift itself nicely over a shoal or along a reef with very little attention. It is also possible to slow the drift by dragging a canvas bucket or sea anchor of some kind. The proper way to fish a drift is downwind, ahead of the boat, and this may be advisable for brown trout and other fish that hold or cruise close to the surface. But for fish that rise from a depth, such as rainbow and cutthroat trout, I have not found it necessary. Casting upwind allows one to use the draw of the boat to keep the line tight and work a livelier fly. If the boat is drifting broadside, as it should be, it also allows one to cast at a considerable angle from the line of the drift and so bring the fly round in a good curve along the trough of the waves or ripples. The same thing can, of course, be done downwind, but with the boat drifting down towards the fly there is seldom time for the cast to straighten out completely and give the change of direction to the fly that so often trips the reaction of a following fish.

SOME LAKE-FISHING PROBLEMS AND METHODS

In lake fishing, as in stream fishing, the fly-fisherman is almost constantly handling line with his left hand. In a lake there is no current to help with the action of his fly, only the movement of the boat if it is drifting or being rowed. When it is anchored or when the fisherman is wading all movement must be created by the lift of the rod or by drawing line in the left hand. Because of this, many authorities have recommended the use of rods at least twelve feet long for lake fishing; but the advice has always been disregarded and I fancy it always will be, if only because shorter rods are so much more convenient and less tiring. I am inclined to think that any fisherman who does most of his fishing in trout lakes would find a light, soft action rod of twelve feet very rewarding. Such a rod gives excellent control in casting, makes roll casting very easy and is a help in striking fish; above all, it does a great deal in working the fly effectively and considerably reduces the need for stripping and coiling line in the left hand.

For the rest of us, who will certainly continue with the eight- and nine-foot rods we use on streams, line handling will continue to be all important. The techniques are not essentially different from those one uses on a stream, but it is probably even more important to vary the techniques until the right one is found.

The sinking line really comes into its own in lake fishing, because it will get the fly down fast and allows a fast, deep recovery. When the fish are feeding at some depth below the surface, as they so often are, this makes for much more satisfactory and more interesting fishing than the rather slow business of waiting for an ordinary line to soak up and sink down. But it is still much less pleasant to lift and cast than a floating line and strikes to a deep fly are not nearly so exciting and satisfying as surface rises. If any fish at all are taking near the surface I prefer a floating line or an intermediate line, even though the bag at the end of the day may be smaller.

A dry fly is often effective on lakes, even in the early spring. It fishes best in a good breeze and nothing is better

under such conditions than a spider on a light leader. Hair
flies are also useful and I have found that very large ones, up
to size 6, will bring really big fish to the surface, especially
in a strong wind. Late evening will nearly always bring a few
fish to the dry fly, except in unseasonably cold weather. In
brown-trout lakes it is often possible to detect the line of a
cruising fish and place a dry fly ahead of him—the same thing
is true of whitefish in big northern lakes on a calm evening.
Rainbow and cutthroat trout seldom cruise faithfully to a
line and are very likely to turn back into deep water after a
rise. Under quiet conditions it is a good idea to cast the fly out,
let it sit briefly, then begin working it back to the boat in a
series of twitches that alternatively drag it and rest it. Both
dry and wet flies will often take very good fish right against
the edges of weed beds or even when cast right in among
standing reeds. Good bass are commonly taken among lily
pads and big trout may be found there at times, though I
have found that these last are likely to be spawners of the
previous season, in poor condition.

Though I am not enthusiastic about two or three flies on a
leader, there is no doubt that this rigging is often effective in
lake fishing, and it is also a useful means of testing one pattern against another. When three flies are fished in this way
the first is called the "point fly," the second "the dropper"
and the third, nearest the line, is the "bobfly." The dropper
and the bobfly are tied into the leader on short points of gut
or nylon. One very deadly method of fishing this rigging is
to hold the rod well up in fishing out the cast so that the fly
nearest the line rides or bobs along the surface; it may be

either a wet or dry pattern, but dry is probably best. A long rod is especially helpful in this type of fishing.

There are times on most lakes, usually in the late evening, when every fish seems to be rising freely at the surface yet very few fish can be taken. I have tried everything I know to solve these rises, but have never succeeded in doing so. It is usually possible to take some good fish on a large silver-bodied wet fly—something powerful enough to draw their attention away from the hatch—but this is no real solution and yields little satisfaction. One can also take occasional fish on very small flies, No. 18 or so, either wet or dry. The fish are feeding on an extremely prolific hatch of small midges and the explanation for their lack of interest in artificial flies is, I am sure, that these become lost in the general abundance that is available in ever direction. If one is taken, it is by virtue and coincidence of being the creature nearest to the fish's mouth at that particular moment. I always enjoy these rises, in spite of their brief duration and frustrating nature. Next time I shall try a silver body and a wisp of white hackle on a No. 20 hook in the hope of attracting attention. Besides, there is always the hope of foul-hooking a fish in perfectly good faith as he boils near your artificial while taking a natural half an inch away.

CHAPTER FIFTEEN

Estuaries and Salt Water

ALMOST ANY salt- or brackish-water fish that feeds on other small creatures can be taken on the fly—or rather on a lure or streamer fly that is cast and worked like a fly. Bonefish and Pacific salmon are two of the outstanding examples, but the list is practically limitless, from rockfish to striped bass, from mackerel to tarpon and tuna.

It goes without saying that a strong, quick rod that will cast a heavy line and a large fly are essential for most of this fishing. Much open-sea fishing is best done by trolling the fly, because many of the fish prefer to follow a longish way before striking. This is even true of the Pacific silver or coho salmon, an excellent fly-rod fish, though there are times when a fly cast and worked from a boat or even from the shore will be taken very promptly and confidently. Long, accurate and skillful casting is necessary for bonefish, which feed in extremely shallow water and are usually very shy.

Any thorough examination of salt-water fly-fishing is beyond the scope of this book, but it seems worth emphasizing that the fishing is usually there for those who want it and will study the ways and needs of the fish. Tackle and techniques need not be very different from those used in fresh-water fishing, though casting demands are likely to be greater in some ways and the tackle should generally be of salmon weight rather than trout weight. A largish reel that will carry up to two hundred yards of backing is desirable, sometimes essential. Non-corrosive reels and rod fittings are important, as is a little special attention to tackle, such as regular oiling of reels and periodic washing of lines in fresh water to get rid of the salt. Hooks also must be washed and dried to prevent rust. It is a good idea to put used flies in a separate box until they have been looked after.

Tides are always important in salt-water fishing, but they are a local matter and any generalization will be unsound. Change of light at dawn and dusk is also likely to be important, as nearly all salt-water life moves at these times in response to the movement of the light-hating planktons. But the importance of this is also subject to wide local variations, and local fishermen and guides are always the most knowledgeable authorities. A local tide book is an essential part of any salt-water fisherman's equipment and just as essential to the estuary fisherman.

Returning salmon and sea trout of all species offer the fly-fisherman excellent opportunities as they enter the tidal reaches of their streams. Most sea trout do not wander very far from the streams that bred them and are likely to return to feed in or just off the estuaries in almost any month of the year, though some months are more favorable than others. The larger estuaries hold sea trout all the time if one can only find them.

To keep the subject within bounds, yet give some idea of its possibilities, it seems best to discuss here only the smaller estuaries that can be fished by wading. These offer the most interesting and satisfying fishing and the movements of the fish are essentially the same as those in the larger estuaries.

All three species of true trouts, the brown, the rainbow and the cutthroat, have sea running races, as do at least three of the chars, the eastern brook trout, the Dolly Varden and the so-called arctic char, and all provide excellent sport.

My own preference in estuary fishing is for the extreme tides, since the fish seem to move and feed better on these, and I would rather fish the last two hours of the ebb tide and the first two hours of the flood than any other time. The stream bed is then clearly revealed across the flats and one can follow it out to the edge of the sea. The water one has to search is limited and the current helps with the search.

Estuary trout feed on a wide variety of underwater creatures, from sow bugs and sand fleas to shrimps and small fish. Sometimes they show readily at the surface, at others they are well down near bottom, but it is nearly always possible to find them by working steadily along the stream channel and trying the fly at different depths and with different actions. A silver-bodied wet fly is one of the best producers, most streamer flies are fairly good and flies like the spruce fly, that have a lively wing action, often catch fish. But one need never be afraid of trying flies as small as size 12 or 14 when fish are difficult to find; the chances are they will be taken just as readily and far more faithfully than anything larger.

At low-water slack there is usually a slight lull in the activity of the fish, but one can often find them again by searching the salt water on either side of the stream mouth. As the tide floods, the fish are likely to move in with it, spasmodically and uncertainly perhaps, but often feeding with quiet determination. Sometimes they turn to gentle surface rises and will then usually respond to a floating fly.

Estuary fishing has many charms and not least among them are the surroundings—the bird life of the flats, the constantly changing currents and water levels, the misty summer dawns and still evenings. The chance of an unusually big fish or some unexpected species is always an exciting possibility. And in streams where salmon run one is never certain whether the next fish will be a ten-pound salmon or a two-pound trout. On one small Pacific Coast estuary I have taken cutthroat trout, Dolly Vardens, coho and pink salmon, coho jack salmon and large rockfish all in a single morning.

The estuary fisherman can, if he wishes, fish right on through the flood tide, as the fish usually continue to move up with it. But they become increasingly difficult to find as there is more water to search, unless one has discovered likely feeding stations upstream. These may be at certain bends of the stream, in pools that fill suddenly with the surge of the tide, around old wharves or pilings, in bays or back eddies. They are found only by watching and searching, but they are worth finding because the fish will pause in them year in, year out, at the same stages of tide and flow. Even at dead low tide, searching is an important part of estuary fishing unless the fish are feeding obviously on some specialized type of feed. It is never wise to spend too long in one spot without some sort of response, nor is it wise to pass up unlikely water without a few trial casts, as the fish are nearly always moving. Even in a place where one has hooked several fish in succession, a quiet spell should suggest a change of place as the fish will very probably have moved on.

All in all, estuary fishing may be considered the least specialized as well as the most interesting form of salt-water fly-fishing and for this reason it is probably the best preparation for all other forms. With reasonable care, all ordinary fresh-water fly-fishing gear can be used in estuary fishing, but it is essential in this case to sponge off rod, reel, line, in fact the whole outfit, in fresh water at the end of the day. Large flies and long casts are not important, but both can be used at times with good effect. Tides are important, as is close study of the movements and feeding habits of the fish, so the estuary fisherman's experience will certainly prove useful elsewhere.

BEACH FISHING

Fly-fishing from rocks and beaches is generally less rewarding than estuary fishing unless one knows the locality very intimately. But it holds plenty of possibilities for the fly-fisherman. Trout and char, as well as salmon, can frequently be found in salt water at some distance from stream mouths and usually take freely when they can be found. Searching them out with the fly can be a slow and tiresome business, so I sometimes carry a casting rod and make a few casts with a small spoon or spinner in each likely place until the fish are found. As soon as a fish strikes at a spinner, one can change over to the fly—usually with good results. But I am not sure that this procedure makes much sense. The casting rod is always at an advantage in fishing from a beach and it seems faintly ridiculous to go out of one's way to accept a handicap. Besides, carrying and caring for two rods is a constant nuisance. Perhaps it is more sensible to accept the casting rod as the right tool for beach fishing, at least until one has established places where the fish feed and can be reached with a fly.

Use of spoon or spinner to find feeding fish by trolling from a boat is much more sensible. Carrying a second rod presents no problem at all and one is under no handicap with the fly once the fish have been found.

The usefulness of salt-water fly-fishing is limited to times when the fish are feeding near the surface. Flats and reefs and shoals have value in salt water exactly as they do in lakes.

But in the sea everything is on a much vaster scale. A good bank for commercial trolling may be forty or fifty fathoms deep, but the fly-fisherman can hope for little if the feed the fish are concerned with is deeper than one or two fathoms. Similarly, fish working on large herring or any similar prey are unlikely to be tempted by the largest of streamer flies, though they may come readily when the herring are only three of four inches long; when feeding on launce fish they will often come to flies on size 6 hooks or smaller, even though the launce fish may be several inches long. Salt-water fish feeding on shrimp can be very difficult for the fly-fisherman, though they can be caught. Flies representing shrimp are, I understand, used with some success for bonefish, and at times they are effective for Pacific salmon.

There is not much doubt that lures of all kinds are generally more effective than flies for highly predatory fish under active feeding conditions. The reason for this is that ordinary flies cannot be—or so far have not been—made to reproduce the erratic wobbling or spinning movements of lures, and it is this erratic movement, either by its visual effect or the vibration it sets up in the water or both, that trips the reaction in the fish and produces the strike. Flies with an attached spinner or blade are too heavy and clumsy to be cast comfortably and the extra weight of swivels to counteract the spinning movement makes casting completely impossible, so few fly-fishermen will bother with them. While I am not altogether satisfied that the possibilities of making a light fly that will give an erratic movement without spinning the line have been fully explored, I think the salt-water fly-fisherman should recognize that he will usually be at some disadvantage. He has to decide for himself whether the pleasure and satisfaction of moving and hooking fish by his favorite method is worth the disadvantage.

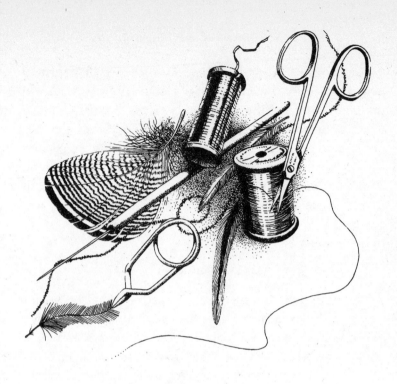

CHAPTER SIXTEEN

The Elements of Fly-Tying

NOT EVERY FLY-FISHERMAN wants to tie his own flies and certainly no one need bother to do so unless he feels like it—flies can be bought in adequate variety for most tastes and most experiments. But many fly-fishermen have some interest in the skills and materials that go into fly-tying and the broad purposes that direct the types and patterns of flies.

Fly-tying is not, in fact, a very difficult performance, nor does it demand any unusual manual dexterity. Almost anyone who wants to try it will find that he can very quickly learn to tie simple, practical flies quite well enough to satisfy the fish. Tying a full-dressed Altantic salmon fly does call for most careful and skillful craftsmanship, and few of us can produce a really elegant and perfectly balanced variant. But a simple strip-wing or hair-wing wet fly, for instance, or a nicely hackled spider are well within the capabilities of anyone who can take a fly reel apart or satisfactorily knot a No. 16 fly to his leader.

FLY-TYING TOOLS

The essential tools of fly-tying are, according to one of my friends who ties far better flies than I do, a pair of scissors, a pair of hackle pliers and a dubbing needle. But most of us also use a simple flytier's vise which clamps on to a table or bench and holds the hook securely, leaving both hands free for the work.

When the hook is firmly clamped in the vise, the first thing is to wax a length of tying silk thoroughly by drawing it back and forth through a piece of cobbler's wax and then wrap it evenly along the shank of the hook from near the eye to a point roughly opposite the barb. This makes the foundation of the fly and the waxed thread ensures that the body and other materials will stay firmly in place.

A SIMPLE DRESSING

To keep everything as simple as possible, assume that the tier has decided to tie a silver-bodied bucktail on a No. 6

hook. He would next take a few short strands of bucktail
hair and tie them in firmly at the tail of the hook with two or
three wraps of the waxed silk. To free his hands for the next
step he would then clamp his hackle pliers to the silk and
leave them hanging down to maintain the tension by their
weight. His next concern is the body material, a length of flat
silver tinsel about one-sixteenth of an inch wide. He would
taper one end of this slightly with his scissors, then tie this
end in, holding it forward along the shank of the hook, towards the eye. Once it is secure he winds the silk on up the
hook to within about one-fourth inch of the eye and leaves
it there with the hackle pliers still holding the tension.

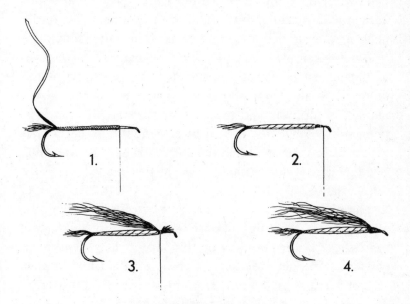

SILVER-BODIED BUCKTAIL

Winding the flat silver tinsel smoothly and evenly up the hook is probably the most difficult part of tying this particular fly. It should not overlap and there should be no gaps. When it reaches the tying silk it is secured again with two or three turns, trimmed off short against the hook, then wrapped a little more—the extra turns of the silk will make a waxed foundation for the hair wing.

The wing is made of some fifteen or twenty strands of bucktail hair just long enough to reach from the eye to the bend of the hook. It is as well to wax the butt end of these, too, before tying them in—the whole clump should be securely held between the thumb and forefinger of the left hand while the thumb and forefinger of the right hand work in the wax. The clump is then placed in position on top of the hook and secured by the tying silk. The butts should be trimmed to an even taper from the silk almost to the eye. This taper is then firmly wrapped with even turns of the tying silk, secured by a whip finish. The remainder of the tying silk is cut away and the head of the fly—the wraps of tying silk holding the wing in place—should be touched up with a little varnish. When the varnish is dry the fly is finished, and even such a simple tying as this one will certainly catch fish.

The purpose of this account is simply to describe the bare mechanics of tying a fly and to show what an easy and logical process it is. No one would want to stop at such an elementary pattern as this, but even so the steps to greater sophistication are not much more difficult. It is almost entirely a matter of getting to know the different materials that produce the various effects and learning their uses. I have purposely omitted the *hackle* from the silver-bucktail dressing I have just described, because hackles are among the most important materials a flytier uses and their best use demands one or two special techniques.

HACKLES AND THEIR USE

The best hackles come from the neck, or sometimes the saddle, of a two-year-old domestic rooster in his spring plumage. These are hard, bright, strongly fibered feathers, long and narrow and tapering to a point. In color, they may vary from the white of the Leghorn to the rich red of the Rhode Island or the English game cock, from the blue of the Andalusian to the grizzled black and white of the Plymouth Rock. Flytiers have special names for most colors and combinations, such as "badger" for the hackle with black center and white tips, "furnace" for black center and red tips, "ginger" and "honey" for the lighter shades of red, but it is not necessary to examine these here.

The chief use of hackle feathers is to make the collar of fibers that stands almost straight out from the hook near the neck of most flies. In wet flies this serves to balance the fly in the water, to add to its movements and to veil the body. The hackles used are generally fairly soft—some tiers prefer those from hens rather than roosters—and are tied to lie somewhat along the hook instead of standing stiffly out from it. For dry flies bright stiff hackles with very fine sharp points to the individual fibers are highly valued, because such hackles contribute greatly to the floating qualities of the fly and rest as lightly on the surface film as the feet of an aquatic insect.

The hackle effect on a fly is produced by winding the hackle round and round the hook in close turns, so that the individual fibers separate and stand out. But the hackle itself must first be prepared in one of two ways, by folding or stripping. Stripping simply means that the fibers are stripped off one side of the quill, so that the remaining fibers will all stand out the same way when the quill is wound on the hook. Folding is a little more difficult. The best way is to clip on two pairs of hackle pliers, one at the tip of the feather, the other on the protruding quill at the butt. Hold the pair on the tip in the left hand, those on the butt in the palm of the right hand. Bend the feather in a semi-circle to separate the fibers, slightly moisten the thumb and middle finger of the right hand and fold the hackle between these. The folding is done by brushing the moistened thumb and finger upwards along the fibers and at the same time smoothing them backwards towards the butt. The bright side of the fibers should be outward. A perfect fold can sometimes be achieved in one smooth continuous movement, but a lot of adjustment is possible and a feather can be folded section by section, with re-moistened fingers if necessary, so long as the quill is kept from twisting on its axis. This may sound difficult and perhaps it is; but with only a limited amount of practice it becomes quite easy.

The next thing is putting the stripped or folded hackle on the hook. The simplest way to describe this to describe the tying of a spider dry fly. Put a No. 16 or No. 14 hook in the vise. Wax a length of fine tying silk and wrap the hook

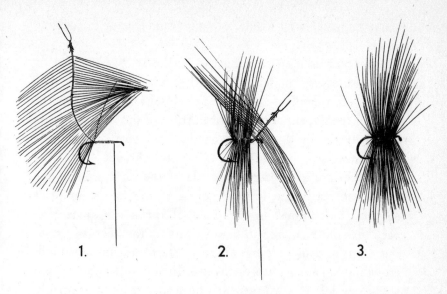

1.   2.   3.

TYING A SPIDER

from just behind the eye to a point opposite the barb. Fold
a suitable hackle and remove the hackle pliers from the tip,
leaving those on the butt. Tie in the tip of the hackle so that
it is pointing forward towards the eye and carry the wrapping
of the silk forward to a point just short of its original start.
Leave it there with hackle pliers holding the tension. Next
wrap the hackle in close even turns along the hook, keeping
the quill always towards the hook shank and smoothing the
fibers of each turn back out of the way of the next turn with
the thumb and forefinger of the left hand. When the turns
bring the quill to the tying silk, strip off any remaining fibers
and tie the quill securely in, finishing the head of the fly with
the usual whip finish and varnishing. The result may not be a

perfect spider, but it will be a fly that can be made to float and catch fish.

The process used in tying the hackle into a standard fly is almost exactly the same except that fewer turns are needed to produce the effect and these are closely grouped near the head of the fly, either behind or in front of the wing. In tying a wet fly the quill is turned on the hook so that the fibers slant backwards instead of sticking straight out. The chief difficulties are in selecting a hackle of the right size for the hook—normally the longest points of the hackle in place should reach almost to the point of the hook—in placing each turn on the hook without catching up the fibers of previous turns and in judging where to start and finish without crowding too much towards the eye. In any well-tied fly room should be left for two turns of the leader to settle in firmly behind the eye of the hook when the fly is knotted on for use.

WING MATERIALS

Whole hackles may also be effectively used as the wings of flies. In wet flies the usual method is to select two matching hackles and tie them in back to back, crimping the quill at the butts by pressure of the thumbnail against the forefinger so that the feather will be placed properly on the hook when it is tied in. Very small hackles or hackle tips are sometimes used as upright or spent wings in dry flies.

The commonest material for wet-fly wings is probably strips or sets of fibers cut from "matched" feathers and set back to back in such a way that they slant gracefully backward along the top of the hook shank. Nearly all feathers

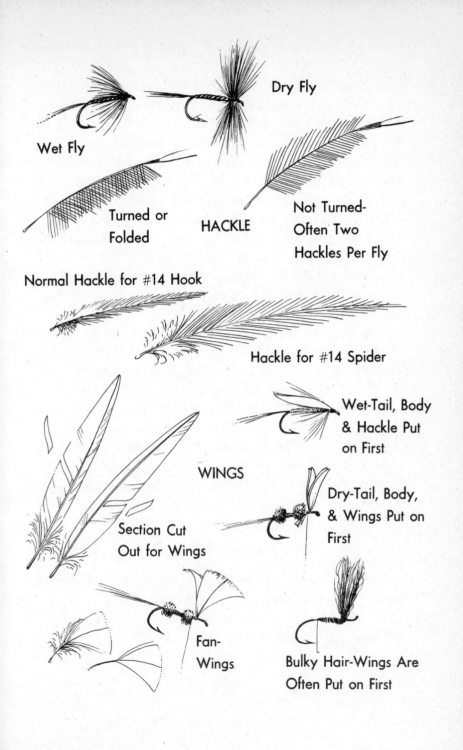

Wet Fly

Dry Fly

Turned or Folded

HACKLE

Not Turned-
Often Two
Hackles Per Fly

Normal Hackle for #14 Hook

Hackle for #14 Spider

WINGS

Section Cut
Out for Wings

Wet-Tail, Body
& Hackle Put
on First

Dry-Tail, Body,
& Wings Put on
First

Fan-
Wings

Bulky Hair-Wings Are
Often Put on First

have longer and more strongly colored fibers on one side of the quill than on the other. Two matched feathers are known as "right-hand" and "left-hand" feathers, because one will have its best fibers on the left of the quill as the good side is held towards the tier, the other on the right. Matching strips are cut from these two opposite sides to make an even pair of strips that can be set smoothly and evenly on the hook.

Among feathers commonly used for winging wet flies are those from mallard (light and dark), teal (heavily barred black and white), wood or summer duck and dyed swan. The center tail feathers of the various pheasants are also excellent. But satisfactory wing strips can be cut from matched feathers of almost any bird.

Hair wings are made from bucktail, polar-bear fur, squirrel tails, moose hair and many other forms of hair and fur, and are used in both wet and dry flies. They are quite easy to use, though some hairs must be well waxed to prevent slipping, and make extremely effective flies. Dry flies with hair wings and tails float better than most ordinary dry flies in rough water and for that reason are especially popular on western streams, though they are also used extensively for trout and Atlantic salmon in the East. The stiffer hairs such as bucktail are especially useful in shaping bass bugs.

BODY MATERIALS

Floss silk, which is available in many excellent colors, is one of the easiest materials to use in making the bodies of flies. It is usually tied in at the tail in the same way as tinsel and wound forward over the waxed silk foundation. But it is considerably easier to put on because, unlike tinsel, it is completely flexible and may be lapped without distorting the smooth shape of the body. Wool and chenille also make good bodies and are easy to put on.

Seal's fur and hare's ear are two popular "dubbings." The individual hairs are short and must be teased out until they can be wound on to the tying silk and carried forward up the body by it. Dubbings give the body a rough effect and are also somewhat more resistant to water than silk or wool or chenille.

Raffia is another useful body material and almost any hair, fur or feather fibers may be worked up and secured to make a special body color or shape. The quills of feathers are used in a number of well-known dry flies such as the Quill Gordon, the Blue Quill and many variants. Tinsel for flytiers may be gold or silver and is available in many shapes and sizes. When a fly is needed to sink quickly, the body is sometimes made of copper wire or the plastic-coated electrician's wire that is available in many colors.

TAILS, TAGS AND BUTTS

This brief description of some of the materials that go into the making of the wings, bodies and hackles of flies gives some idea of the variety available to the flytier. It must be added that still more variety can be and is achieved by mixing body materials, wing materials and even hackles. In some flies, especially dry flies, tails may be important and again a great variety of materials may be used. Many tiers like to add finish to their flies by a "tag" of colored silk or tinsel wire set just behind the tail. A few well-known flies such as the Royal Coachman, the Red Ant and the Black Ant are tied with "butts" of peacock or ostrich herl, sometimes referred to as "tips" or "egg sacs." In addition certain short, strongly marked feathers, such as the eyed jungle cock, may be tied in outside the wings, when they are known as "sides," and even smaller feathers such as blue chatterer and Indian crow may be tied outside these again as "cheeks."

This enormous variety both in the materials of fly-tying and the way they are used may well seem absurd and from the point of view of any one individual flytier I think it is absurd. Most of us use only a limited range of materials and ring quite enough changes on these. But flytiers since the beginning of time have been looking for flies that the fish will find irresistible under certain conditions, if not all conditions. It seems a worthy search, however irrational. And there is also the challenge of craftsmanship, the search for grace of form and subtle beauty of color, that the really skillful tier is bound to feel. This, too, is worthy and it is wholly rational as well. But the beginning flytier should limit himself to a few standard materials and a few simple patterns until he is able to turn out flies that are neat and well shaped and will hold together under fishing conditions. Having achieved this, he will inevitably try out more difficult materials and the irresistible pattern will seem almost within reach. Occasionally, when some new creation is tried out on a particularly good day, it may even seem to have been attained. If disappointment follows later, as it inevitably must, it matters little. Catching a fish on a pattern of one's own tying and conception is always a flattering and satisfying experience.

CHAPTER SEVENTEEN

Some Esoteric Points

WHILE I HAVE conscientiously tried to keep this book to the simple essentials of fly-fishing, I know I have allowed references to many of the finer points to creep in. This is, I think inevitable, because so much of the charm of fly-fishing is in the way it leads one on to more ambitious techniques and more intricate understanding of fish and their ways.

I should like to make it clear that there is abundant pleasure to be found in understanding and using the basic tackle and techniques of fly-fishing, that many men have not merely found these sufficient but have made themselves into redoubtable fishermen with no more than this and their own powers of observation and deduction. In other words it is essentially a simple sport and no one should feel bound to encumber himself with anything beyond its simplicities. It is a pleasure, a recreation, a delight, something to be enjoyed, not an obsession or a duty or a driving force. But if it beckons on into the mazy paths of higher theory and finer practice and the simple fisherman feels inclined to respond, there is no slightest reason why he should not do so, and every possible reason why he should.

Fortunately, fly-fishing has an outstanding literature and any fly-fisherman who wants to advance in the sport will find many fine books to lead him on in the line of any specialization he cares to adopt. He will find also a fair number that entertain and satisfy by their quality and style alone. And finally there are those which so expertly describe specific types of fishing, even though under far different conditions than those familiar to the reader, that they both entertain and instruct.

One of the most attractive modern books on fly-fishing is the late John Atherton's *The Fly and the Fish*. It is a very clear book, beautifully illustrated by the author himself and, though quite short, it deals expertly with fly-fishing all across North America. Atherton was a good artist and a good fly-fisherman, with a keen, inquiring mind and a deep love of the sport and its traditions; he raises and explains many points of real interest to any experienced fisherman and his approach throughout is just what is needed to stimulate the reader to constructive thinking of his own.

Theodore Gordon is a much less recent American writer, but he, too, is a fisherman's fisherman, full of thoughts and theories and practical ideas. His notes and letters, edited by John McDonald into a fine thick volume called *The Complete Fly Fisherman,* is a wonderful companion for any fly-fisherman, young or old; and it has the additional advantages of traditional and historical significance, since Gordon is properly regarded as the father of modern American fly-fishing.

Ray Bergman is a friendly writer, catholic in his fishing tastes and very comprehensive. His three books, *Trout, Just Fishing,* and *With Fly, Plug, and Bait,* cover almost every aspect of North American fresh-water fishing and provide the most extensive lists of flies and fly dressings I know.

E. R. Hewitt's *Secrets of the Salmon* and *Telling on the Trout,* with George M. La Branche's *Dry Fly and Fast Water,* are books that every North American fly-fisherman should read, for these two were true masters, persistent, ingenious and immensely skillful. Both were men who studied fish closely and developed streamcraft to a fine point, and their influence is to be found at work wherever a fly is cast or fly-fishermen gather to discuss their sport.

Of the many admirable British writers, Frederic M. Halford is important still, though he wrote almost half a century ago, for his meticulous development of dry-fly fishing and G. E. M. Skues for his equally conscientious development of nymph fishing. Both, like Hewitt and La Branche, were masters and most of what they wrote still stands up, in spite of changes and improvements in tackle. Although Halford's specialization was intense and his views were often narrow, every dry-fly fisherman owes much to him, and most can still learn much from him. Skues, besides being a charming writer, was highly original and adaptable and he had a profound understanding of the ways and moods of fish.

J. W. Hills, Lord Grey of Fallodon and H. Plunket Greene, the singer, are others who wrote beautifully and informatively of English chalk-stream fishing, and Hills is particularly interesting because of his thorough knowledge of the long history of fly-fishing. One of his books, *A History of Fly Fishing for Trout,* outlines the literature and traditions of fly-fishing and gives the reader a keen sense of the centuries of gradual development that have produced the fine shades of technique we use today. Even without urging from Hills, most fly-fishermen like to turn back to Charles Cotton, the friend of Izaak Walton who wrote the fly-fishing section of *The Compleat Angler.* But Hills calls attention to many books and many writers, some of them earlier than Cotton.

There are plenty of good fishing books besides those I have mentioned here, and more are written every year. Some cover specific local conditions and may well have a more direct appeal for the fishermen who live in those localities than the books I have mentioned. It would not be easy to select among them, nor is it really necessary, since they are sure to be well known locally. But one recent book of universal interest is Charles Ritz's *A Fly Fisher's Life.* Charles Ritz is a fine fisherman, an expert designer of rods and other gear and a man of immense and lively enthusiasm. He has fished almost everywhere in the world and always with a quick, intelligent and wide-open mind. His book is beautifully illustrated and full of every kind of excitement from beginning to end.

The reading fisherman, or even one who just talks a lot with his fellows, will soon find himself wondering how there can possibly be so many conflicting theories so firmly held by so many expert people. The explanation is, of course, that we none of us really know very much about the essential thing—that is, just how and why and when fish move and feed—so we are bound to theorize. Then we test our theories in the only way we can, by trial and error under actual fishing conditions, with all the limitations of our own particular habits, skills and preconceived notions. Sometimes we are successful, so we boldly expound our theory until something else comes up to modify or change it. I have mentioned that Hewitt and La Branche held radically different theories about the proper length of leaders. Halford once said to Skues, in a famous London club: "You know, young man, those things you wrote about in your book just can't be done." Skues answered: "But I know they can be done. I've done them." Skues was right, of course, but Halford, obsessed with the perfections of the dry fly, simply would not believe in the possibilities of the nymph, and to the end of their lives these two great experts never did get together on the matter.

This brings me squarely to the question of the purist. Halford was a dry-fly purist—he would fish nothing but a floating fly under any circumstances, and that only to a rising fish. Since he had personally developed the method to its present perfection and fished only on streams that favored it, he had every possible right to his preference and to the title he cheerfully accepted for himself and his colleagues—the "ultra-

173

purists." Dry-fly purists, he said, were those who would sometimes cast to a fish found in a feeding position, but not actually seen to rise. Halford's obsession with the dry fly largely blinded him to what goes on under the water and enabled him to write of nymph fishing three years after Skue's book *Minor Tactics* was published: "Candidly I have never seen this method in practice, and I have grave doubts as to its efficacy."

Purity in this degree stems from prejudice rather than conviction and is plainly limiting, but it doesn't change the fact that Halford's theories worked out and still work out on chalk streams everywhere when conditions are right for them—which is most of the time. Nor does it change the fact that Skues' ideas were completely sound when conditions were right for them. Both men were great experts and great fishermen, but both would have had to modify their theories had they fished at all extensively in North America.

The trout of the English chalk streams, on which so much fly-fishing lore is based, are brown trout; the streams themselves are quiet rippling flows of clear water over weed beds and gravel beds that produce great quantities of feed, both under water and on the surface. For the most part the trout hover quietly in favorite feeding stations, bulging to the underwater nymph movements or gently intercepting the drifting May flies as the current carries them into the chosen places. Similar conditions can be found in North America and the trout respond to them in much the same way; but they are unusual. Most of our streams are rockier, faster, more broken and less fertile. Abundant surface hatches are rare; both rises and fish are hard to see; the fish are less faithful to their feeding stations, they rise less confidently and deliberately, frequently coming from well down in the water and turning back into the depths immediately from the rise. This could, in fact, be said to be the normal behavior of both cutthroat and rainbow trout in fast streams and I have noticed that brown trout seem to adopt much the same habits in the fast-water streams of the Pacific Coast and on both slopes of the Andes.

All these differences, as Theodore Gordon quickly found, called for different techniques, and North American fishermen have been inventing and testing different equipment and techniques ever since his time. All are, of course, modifications of the orthodox wet- and dry-fly methods that came from across the Atlantic, but they are extreme enough to amount to seeming contraditions, especially in the West.

In the light of all this the terms "purist" and "ultra-purist" in the sense that Halford used them simply do not exist. They imply a conservatism and narrowness that no North Americans could possibly wish to practice. There are a few North Americans who will fish nothing but a floating fly and there are many, many more who limit their fishing to fly-fishing. But neither limitation can imply any narrowly conservative approach if the fisherman is to be reasonably effective under diverse conditions.

In my opinion the really good fly-fisherman is the man who can use dry fly, nymph and wet fly in all their forms as the conditions call for them. Few of us have time for more than this, but if we have I know of no reason in the world why we shouldn't throw hardware or return to the worms of our youth or fish in any other way we choose. There is pleasure in all of them and much to be learned from most of them. But it remains true that the trout and salmon of North America, and a good many other fish as well, can be persuaded to take a fly of some sort under most conditions. When they do so the rewards, in terms of sport and interest, are richly satisfying. To take such fish by less satisfying means has always seemed to me a waste of sport.

CHAPTER EIGHTEEN

Ethics and Aesthetics

T HERE IS, I think, not much point in being a fly-fisherman unless one is prepared to be generous and fairly relaxed about it all. Competition has no place at the streamside. One's purpose is not to do better than some other fisherman, but to get response from the fish and learn something about them, and both of these objectives are best achieved by the concentration of a relaxed mind.

The whole idea of skill in casting, sound equipment and

a good knowledge of techniques is to free the mind for the pleasure of fishing. True, there is pleasure in casting, conscious pleasure in the proper use of techniques, even in the handling of good equipment, but all these are the background of going fishing. One enjoys them, whether the fish are there or not, but they should never intrude. If the skills have been mastered, if they are used naturally, almost instinctively, they will not intrude, but will simply provide greater freedom for enjoyment.

The generosity I am thinking of is an attitude, a whole approach to the whole subject. It implies generosity to other fishermen, to the fish themselves, to the water and surroundings in which they live. It is something a fly-fisherman can well afford and, by affording it, add greatly to his pleasure and relaxation.

Generosity to other fishermen is, I suppose, no more than common courtesy, but it should be a matter of feeling as well as practice. On private waters where fishermen are few, this should come easily enough, but on public waters that are more or less heavily fished it may require rather more conviction. Yet the logic of "do as you would be done by" has even stronger application on public than on private waters.

The first courtesy should be to respect another fisherman's privacy—that is, to avoid crowding him, to give him room to follow through his normal fishing plan. On streams this means that one should avoid entering too closely below a fisherman who is working downstream or too closely above one working upstream; better still, enter below the man who is fishing upstream and above the one who is working down. On lakes it is wrong to crowd a boat out of its planned drift, to cut in ahead of a boat working the shoreline or to anchor too close to another anchored boat. To those who fish extremely crowded waters, these may seem impossible counsels, but in my experience they are not. An opening weekend or some other special occasion may make difficulties, but even at such times the tendency is to crowd certain particular places and the mildest of non-conformists can avoid these. If he does, he usually finds less cluttered water, perhaps of less repute, but at least as likely to yield a fish or two as any of the pestered pools. On more normal occasions it is often simply a matter of waiting and watching while a single fisherman, or at most two or three, fish through a pool. If they fish well, these is pleasure in watching them; if they fish badly there is the slightly less respectable pleasure of noting the likely places that are passed by; and in either event there is a surprisingly good chance of finding fish when one's own turn comes. I have fished a dry fly upstream all day while meeting an unending downstream flow of spinners, bait fishermen and wet-fly fishermen and still had a respectable catch to show for it.

On lakes it is much the same. One may not be able to get into some favorite spot or drift, but it can happen that one finds an even more productive place as a result. Similarly, one can often wait out several fishermen who have anchored over a lively shoal, move in when they have gone and find plenty of fish there still. Angling at its most deadly is seldom such an efficient means of catching fish that nothing is left.

If one happens to be in fortunate possession of a pool or a good stretch of water when other fishermen arrive, the reasonable thing is to fish it out with care, but without unnecessary delay or disturbance and surrender it promptly and graciously. Lasting friendships can be made in this way. If the new arrivals are unkind enough to push in immediately ahead, it is often possible to give them time to widen the gap and then work on successfully. If they happen to be static bait fishermen, the only thing is to go around, giving them a wide berth for their own activities. Only occasionally is the invasion so impossibly vigorous that there is nothing left but to reel in and move on.

It is ordinary waterside courtesy to give, freely and honestly, whatever assistance or advice another fisherman may ask for. Let him know if you have found a particular fly successful and offer him a sample if he has nothing like it. Tell him anything you know of the peculiarities of the lake or stream or of likely places to fish. Offer to help in netting a fish if the occasion arises. But remember, too, that in the matter of unsolicited advice, it is more generous to receive than to give. Unless it happens that your local knowledge is complete, your wisdom flawless and your particular piece of information certain to produce the desired result, it is better to wait to be asked for it.

It is always an important courtesy to disturb the fish and the water as little as possible, so that any fisherman following behind will have a fair chance, and this obligation is redoubled on waters where fish are unusually shy and sophisticated. A competent fly-fisherman should be able to put a succession of flies over a difficult fish and leave him still in position when he gives up.

This, perhaps, is also an expression of generosity to the fish. If one isn't good enough to take him, why disturb his pleasant affairs by clumsy persistence? But there are others, even more important. Of all fishermen, the fly-fisherman needs fewest fish to complete his day. To him, every fish taken should be an affair of interest. He can afford to be selective and usually his chosen method allows him to be selective. A limit, if there is one, should be a meaningless figure, except that it may not be exceeded. He may occasionally wish to take a limit of fish, if he has a use for them. More often two or three fish of good size will make his day. More than that will be a burden rather than a blessing. Occasionally he may prefer to kill no fish at all, but his sport need never suffer for this; he can catch a dozen if he wishes and return them all safely to the water, secure in the knowledge that if he uses reasonable care all are likely to survive to provide sport for someone else.

But if a fish is to be killed, it should be killed promptly and efficiently, by a smart rap on the base of the skull, not left to flop and flounder until it dies. And if a fish is to be returned to the water it should be freed with all possible care and an absolute minimun of handling. If, as very rarely happens with the fly, it is hooked deep in the gullet or if it is bleeding heavily from a wound in the gills, it should probably not be returned.

Occasionally, on closely managed water, there may be a duty to kill fish for the good of the fishery. If so, it is a duty to be respected. But very few public waters indeed are so closely managed that killing fish is a necessity, and usually there are plenty of killers available anyway.

Yet this point does bring up the fisherman's final and most important obligation to the fish, which is to respect his environment, to protect it to the best of his ability and to fight for it if necessary, which it usually is. Good fishing is being destroyed all over North America and the destruction is always unnecessary. When streams and lakes are damaged it is almost invariably the result of bad planning and bad management in the use of other resources. Clean waters, unobstructed waters and undepleted waters are in the long-term interest of everyone; only the shortest of short-term interests are ever served by pollutions, however caused, by temporary diversions, by obstructions that do not allow for adequate fish passage or by the sort of land use that permits silting and causes floods in winter and low flows in summer. If he respects his sport, a fisherman will learn to understand such things and to make his voice clearly heard. There are few better ways of doing this than by actively supporting some local rod and gun club.

This respect for the fish's environment, in my own humble opinion, extends far beyond the water itself. It takes in all the creatures and growth under the water or on the water or along the banks. It extends far out into the countryside, into the meadows and swamps, up into the high mountains where the streams have their origin. It implies not merely a concern for such things and a desire to protect them, but a positive affection for the whole natural world and a deep desire to understand it.

I have no wish, for instance, to consider such beautiful creatures as mergansers and herons and water ouzels, otter and mink and bears competitive predators for my sport. They belong where they are, they have their place and part and it is very rarely indeed that some unnatural factor allows them to increase to an excessive abundance that needs control. I have no special urge to cut away brush and tree limbs that make casting more difficult, for I learned long ago that these often make the places that shelter the best fish.

Fishing is a sport and a relaxation because it offers a man the ideal means of self-realization through close and peaceful identification with his surroundings. Awareness is an important part of this, and so is understanding. Any fisherman needs to concentrate, a fly-fisherman perhaps more than most. But there is always time to forget rod and line and fly and look at other things. It is time well spent, if understanding grows. Every bird and mammal, every insect and weed and tree that can be recognized and named is something added to a man's stature. Every link between them, every change of stream bed or flow, every little thing observed and understood adds to the self-realization, emphasizes the fisherman's identification with his special world. A large part of a fisherman's pleasure should be in these things. In making it so, he will make himself a better fisherman, even though he may kill fewer fish.

INDEX